Kindness will save the WORLD

For all the friends, family, and teachers
whose kindness made me who I am.

And in loving memory of my mother,
Cindy Crews (1958-2022).

Kindness will save the WORLD

Stories of compassion and connection

James Crews

MANDALA

San Rafael Los Angeles London

CONTENTS

Remember there's no such thing as a small act of kindness.
Every act creates a ripple with no logical end.

—Scott Adams

INTRODUCTION

The new year began with an act of kindness. Having just taken a grueling twenty-five hour bus ride across Argentina the day before, my husband, Brad, and I walked the dusty shoulder of a busy highway in Bariloche, searching out fresh produce in that place in Patagonia where we were staying for the next few weeks. We'd underestimated how far our rented cabin was from the center of town—about ten miles or more—and so, without a car or bikes, we were confined to our immediate area. As the warm midday December sun bore down on us, and the deep blue water of the Río Negro shimmered in the distance, we looked for a small, natural-foods store we'd seen on the map.

"There it is," Brad pointed, both of us relieved.

But the market was barely as large as a room when we came upon it, and I was disappointed not to find some of our staples, like oatmeal and honey. Still, we managed to pick out fresh carrots and peppers, some apples, oranges, and bananas just before a woman and her young daughter entered the market, flipping on the lights and turning on some music. As we stacked our produce on the counter, I noticed the woman, who apparently spoke no English, slicing into a ripe honeydew and handing her daughter a piece. Before I knew it, she was wordlessly holding out slices of the melon to each of us, too, sweet juice dripping down as she passed them over the counter, nodding for us to take them.

Because we'd been dealing with waitresses and locals who seemed dismissive of tourists in that breathtaking part of Patagonia, her unexpected kindness nearly brought me to tears. I couldn't help but smile and give a little bow, offering a poorly pronounced "Gracias" as I bit into that delicious melon. In the safety and predictability of my own privileged life in America, I often forget how stressful and exhausting it can be to move through a new culture where the simplest customs baffle you, and where you don't speak enough of the language to communicate even basic needs. Being in a situation like this always strips us down to our most essential elements and brings us to a place of vulnerability most of us would rather spend our lives avoiding. Yet, as the woman showed me that day in Argentina, the pain of feeling like an outsider, of feeling that we don't belong, can be instantly dissolved by some kind gesture that costs almost nothing, but means so much to the receiver because it restores a sense of self-worth, of being seen and valued by another human being.

Once we finished our slices and were ready to pay, the woman held out her hand to collect the rinds and toss them away. "Muchas gracias," I said once again, to which she replied, "De nada." But in that moment, when a little empathy was all we needed to keep us going, it was not nothing. Her gift meant the world to me, and it sent out ripples, as every kindness does, far beyond the initial connection. Perhaps that's why, just a few months after we returned to the US and found ourselves in the grip of a global pandemic that restricted all travel and kept us housebound for months, this moment of tenderness kept coming back to me, still so vivid and real. I strive to be a grateful and positive person, yet as news of the virus worsened and our future looked more chaotic and bleak, I found that the lifelong anxiety I'd been able to keep under wraps the past few years came roaring back. Nothing I did—not long walks in the woods, sitting on my meditation cushion, or talking with my therapist and friends—seemed to offer more than a fleeting sense of relief. The idea of braving the grocery store or pharmacy left me filled with a debilitating fear most days.

Yet as the pandemic wore on, and I ventured more and more into the world again, I found what kept me going were moments of connection shared between strangers and loved ones alike. I started writing down my experiences like this nearly every day, not realizing at the time that I was keeping a kindness journal. I only wanted to preserve the positive and uplifting instances I found in the midst of the most challenging days. We're so bombarded with alarming and frightening news on an hourly basis, it can be hard to trust that goodness remains our basic nature. But what I noticed in the people I encountered, when I was present enough, seemed to prove otherwise. It might have been watching a mother tickle her toddler in a grocery cart, their giggles filling the parking lot, or making a phone call to my oldest friend just to let her know I was thinking about her. The more we look for connections, the more we find them, and the more we begin to create moments of closeness ourselves. Kindness toward yourself is just as essential as tenderness toward others. We sometimes believe that self-care is an indulgence or pure selfishness, when just the opposite is true. Whether springing for a book I was dying to read, or taking ten minutes to sit alone with a cup of licorice tea, anything I did for myself also counted as a kindness, and it helped to keep a record of those times when I'd been good to myself, too.

We forget that kindness is also a key component of mindfulness. In my teaching over the past few years, I have found the need over and over to emphasize mindfulness as an essential act of self-care and potent form of self-love. If we're not able to pause and pay nonjudgmental attention to what's going on in our lives, and to the many moments that might otherwise pass us by, it becomes that much harder to be kind to ourselves—or anyone else for that matter. Perhaps we all need to remember that, as teachers often explain to children, mindfulness has two wings. One is being in the moment, and the other is kindness. Using both of these practices at once can help us steady our lives and minds, and can keep us out of the fear and despair that threaten to overtake us so often these days.

My hope is that by reading these short essays, you'll see the many ways that kindness fills your life, and that you might even feel inspired to keep a kindness journal of your own. Sometimes, we have to look harder, celebrate the smallest of victories, and capture those times we want to keep for later. At various points in the book, I have also included Kindness Practices, which you can simply read through and reflect on, or use as a part of your own writing and journaling. As it turns out, science confirms what I've found to be true about kindness. Social psychologist and author of *Positivity*, Dr. Barbara Fredrickson, has worked to redefine love as "that micro-moment of warmth and connection that you share with another living being." She goes on to point out that "Positivity opens us. The first core truth about positive emotions is that they open our hearts and our minds, making us more receptive and more creative." As you read about the various ways I've absorbed such instants of warmth and love, I hope you'll feel invited to find a similar openness, reaping the benefits of a fuller presence in this beautiful, difficult world we share together.

PART ONE
THE SPARK OF CONNECTION

Sparks

Perhaps community is a constellation. Each one of us is a light in the emerging collective brightness.

—John O'Donahue

I was visiting friends in Chicago, and because they were both at work, I went out to explore their neighborhood, to absorb as much as I could of the early sunshine. After walking for several miles in the bustle of a Sunday morning, I ducked into a coffee shop for juice and a scone. The young man behind the counter smiled at me as he took my money, and his face softened, opening up when he saw that I was smiling back at him as few people do in that rushed and time-bound city.

"How's your morning treating you?" he asked. His words seemed to break through some barrier, and it was as though an actual current now ran through a conduit stretched between us—a charge that had nothing to do with attraction and everything to do with simple connection between people. I was reminded as we chatted why we call it "striking up" a conversation, since if the words we share are authentic, talk with a stranger can be like rubbing two chips of flint together, making sudden sparks that might someday become something more.

I carried his smiling face with me through the rest of my day, all the more willing because of our exchange to offer a smile to others. We easily forget when someone has been kind to us (and tend to remember when someone has wronged or slighted us), so it's good practice to relive an honest connection over and over, to write it down, or tell others about it in order to prolong that feeling of deeper kinship. And if we are positively affected by someone's kind words or smile, if we carry that charge for hours after, we can remember how easily we might change someone else's life by some simple act of care. After all, connection—any exchange with another living being, be it animal, plant, or human—is why we're here. Even the smallest moments open the door for future relationships. They remind us that our actions, and the moments they create, always matter.

When I am at my worst, convinced that what I do affects no one and could never improve the life of another, I make myself take a walk and force myself to smile at everyone I pass. Or I call a good friend and own the vulnerability of needing some positive interaction. Sometimes, if we venture outside our zones of safety into new places and social situations, what we deeply need may just find us, may meet us with a smile that says there will never be anything that can cut us off from the current of kindness that runs through us all.

Oasis

Only connect.

—E. M. Forster

Brad and I had just dropped his mother off at the airport, and as we drove home that rainy morning, wending our way through the traffic in Albany, New York, it began to sleet. And because each of us was already yawning, we pulled off at the coffee shop in the strip mall with its steamed-over windows, looking like a warm, brightly lit oasis in the middle of all that predawn darkness.

We ducked the falling ice and entered that buzzing world where people rushed in and out of as they got ready for work or the coming holiday, barely taking a moment to look each other in the eye. After we eased through the crowd and got our drinks, I stood at the counter, pouring half-and-half into my Americano and stirring slowly with one of those slim wooden sticks. I could feel a woman right behind me waiting for me to finish with the cream, and so, when I was done, I smiled and handed her the cool metal pitcher. She instantly smiled back and said, "Thank you!" as if it was the nicest thing anyone had done for her in ages. Perhaps it was.

For whatever reason, an immediate sense of peace came over me. Maybe the fact that I had acknowledged her existence, that I had not ignored her, brightened the rest of what would have been a very dour Christmas Eve for her. Maybe she needed that bit of interaction as much as I did, and we simply shared the light, making our own little oasis inside the noisy café as day began to break outside.

Saved by Kindness

On the first warmer day in February, Brad and I set out walking on our normal route along the dirt roads near the new house we're building. I could feel the frozen gravel finally softening beneath my boots with each new step, and I kept breathing in the scent of the earth briefly waking up as if to remind us: yes, spring will come again. I looked over at Brad, both of our coats unzipped, gloves stuffed in our pockets, and told him we should keep going.

We headed down to Tink's Pond where, in summer, we often check for muskrats and turtles, who make their homes under the bridge. We leaned over the railing and peered into the clear and running water, relishing the burbling music of all that snowmelt rushing through. On the way back, we spotted a familiar green Toyota truck pulling up next to us. It was Andrew, the owner of the organic farm that Brad helps manage. He had just gone birding near the Battenkill River, he said, then stopped off for doughnuts.

He held up a white bag. "I have an extra, guys," he said, rattling off all the possible flavors we could choose from—chocolate-chocolate, raspberry jelly, cinnamon sugar.

I claimed the cinnamon, and he handed over our doughnut through his open window. Brad and I took turns biting into that deep-fried goodness, which melted in our mouths, sugar already buzzing in my veins as we chatted with Andrew.

"Hey, boys!" said two women who walked up behind us—a couple from New York City who had just bought a house in the neighborhood. We stood back and brought them into the conversation for a few minutes, all of us marveling at the 50-degree day, the suddenly powerful sun doing its work to melt the icy white world around us.

What amazed me more, however, as we said goodbye to them and then to Andrew, was how at home I felt in that instant. Who takes a walk and expects to meet several friends along the way, one of whom offers you a still-warm doughnut fresh from the bakery? It never would have crossed my mind to feel uncomfortable standing there next to Brad, his arm draped over my shoulder, or to feel fearful and threatened while walking those roads as two gay men, our love visible to everyone. Instead, I felt welcomed by each moment we spent chatting with our friend, and with the women who obviously were drawn to our small Vermont village as well. As we feasted on the last of our doughnut, I thought about all the men, women, and LGBTQ+ people in the world for whom this was not the case, who did not feel safe even walking out their doors and being themselves. Growing up in a small town in Missouri, I would never have dreamed of a life as open as this with the man I love. Even going to graduate school in Nebraska, once while innocently walking to the pharmacy, I had been yelled at by boys in a pickup after a football game. I'll never forget the homophobic insults they hurled at me that day.

I can still remember shaking my head in disbelief, feeling chills climb my spine, when I first learned about Brad's history, too. He and I met on a dating app called OkCupid not long after I moved to the East Coast to teach at a community college in Boston. I was weary of online dating at that point, but had come across the profile of this gorgeous man staring into the camera with the kindest eyes I'd ever seen. When I saw that he was an organic farmer living in Vermont, I thought his profile must be fake—he sounded too good to be true. But I sparked up a conversation with him anyway, not expecting much, just telling him how much I enjoyed what he wrote about himself and his attempts to be a better person each day. He responded with the longest message I'd ever received from someone on a dating app, and which I later discovered he had tapped out on his phone. He told me about life on the farm, even confessing that years ago he had been discharged from the Air Force when he was nineteen years old for being gay, under the disastrous "Don't Ask, Don't Tell" policy still in place when he entered the military. He said he came back home with so much shame, it would be years before he admitted the real reason he left the Air Force to anyone else in his family or friend group.

Later on, he told me, because of the intensity of the shame and loss of purpose, for a long time he felt suicidal each and every day, even going so far as to choose which tree he would run his car into when things became unbearable. But it was the kindness of this community that saved him. On the worst days, when he thought he could go on no more, the people driving past him, on the roads where he ran or walked, would smile and wave. They would stop to chat, just as Andrew had that day, and make him feel seen again. When I first read all this in Brad's message, I was struck by his extreme vulnerability in sharing something so personal, as if he could somehow sense, even across the miles that separated us, even on a dating app, of all places, that I would receive the news with tenderness and an open heart. Something in his confession cemented our connection and told me this was a man I wanted to meet and get to know.

Oftentimes, walking these same dirt roads together, I send a silent thank-you to all the people in our village who had no idea that, through their small, seemingly insignificant acts of kindness, they were helping to save his life. I said it again under my breath that day—*thank you, thank you*—as our boots sank in the muddy ruts and we climbed the hill to the house that would soon become our home, unafraid to link arms, hold hands, or brush a kiss across each other's mouths still dusted with cinnamon and sugar.

A Meeting of the Eyes

It was just the slightest kindness, a little wink of light like the last ember in a fire going out, but it was enough to keep me lit for the rest of the day. In the middle of running errands—filling the car with gas, mailing off packages, picking up books from the library, and buying birdseed—my last stop was the bank, where I pulled up next to the slim tube that would send my checks inside for deposit. I love actually going into the bank, standing in line, and seeing other people tending to their money, the tellers sometimes joking with one another, the cheap holiday-of-the-moment decorations and tchotchkes adorning each teller's station. I love the bustle and almost blindingly bright cleanness of the bank, but I also appreciate the convenience of the drive-through on busy days like this.

A teller I didn't recognize greeted me as the tube bearing my checks and deposit slip shot up into the bank. "How are you doing?" she asked in that genuine tone, and we began our small exchange. A huge truck pulled up next to me in the opposite lane, blocking my view of the window. But that didn't stop my teller from coming over to where I could see her, standing on her tiptoes, and meeting my eyes with her eyes as she said, "You're all set. You enjoy the rest of your day."

It wasn't the words that stayed with me, but what she said with that gesture of leaning so I could see her over the hood of the truck, what she said with the effort she made to ensure that our eyes met when she wished me a joyful day. *I mean it,* her attention seemed to say, *and I want you to know it.* She went the extra mile—or perhaps an extra few inches, in this case—to acknowledge me as a human, to make me feel as if my presence was important to her.

You might think there's no way I could get all that from a simple meeting of the eyes. But when you grow accustomed to receiving the opposite, when all the other people you've encountered in your day treat you ever-so-slightly like an object passing through their lives—in line at the grocery store, or on the other side of the post office counter, handing you your receipt as if you're a nameless machine—then you become attuned to every gesture and word that says otherwise, that confirms your humanness, and gives you a sense of belonging. So I drove away with a smile and a wave, just a little startled by the sliver of unexpected attention, reminded again—Is it really so easy to forget the lesson?—that it takes so little to make each other feel real. That moments of exchange like these are the only currency we need.

Nor'easter Blessing

When I'm locked in worry and anxiety, it's looking outside of myself and noticing the small things that lifts me out of the darkness. Seeing red buds on the maple trees or yellow petals bursting forth on the forsythia bush after an endless winter reminds me of rhythms and cycles larger than myself and my own personal suffering. This does not mean I deny my pain or push it aside, just that I allow myself to feel reassured by the relentless energy of the world pressing onward.

This was how it worked for me the other morning. An overnight nor'easter left us with six inches of snow piled up around the house, and I lay awake in bed looking out at headlights cutting through the predawn darkness along the highway, worried about the state of our country and the world. Shifting again with a sigh and trying not to wake Brad, I turned to see my father-in-law in his big maroon truck parked at the end of our driveway with his plow blade raised, about to carve us a path so we could make our way out into the new day. I watched him back up his truck and then push forward over and over, the yellow light blinking on top of his cab like a beacon.

I'd been ruminating on all the negative news I'd read the day before, but his loving gesture pulled me back to the present. *Bless you*, I said under my breath, staring through the window by our bed and thinking of his steady hands on the wheel, marked by years of carpentry. I imagined the steam curling up from the lip of the plastic lid over his cup of gas-station coffee and felt glad that he always makes our house the first stop on his rounds of plowing in town. In the past, I'd have been annoyed to look out and see my father-in-law plowing our driveway or mowing the grass when we didn't ask him to, but these days, I take my kindness wherever I can find it. Life becomes easier when we see the people around us as mostly welcoming and helpful.

Even when they seem to prove us wrong, we can do our best to recognize every small goodness offered to us when we feel the heavy drapes of fear and cynicism dropping over us again. In her poem "Sometimes," Mary Oliver sums up the rules for living well: "Pay attention. Be astonished. Tell about it." When we notice and name those tender moments, we are able to hold onto them more often and are much more likely to find them again in the future.

The Rash

I don't know what made me ask the pharmacist about treatment for the rash on my arm. As I stood at the counter with the plexiglass barrier between us and he passed my prescriptions to me through the small slot, I sensed that we both craved some deeper connection. And after I asked about the red patch on my arm, I watched his eyes light up with the thrill of being needed. I also really *saw* him for the first time, noticing his closely cropped crew cut and the US Air Force button pinned to the lapel of his white coat. The truth was, he had the reassuring look of someone who wanted to help and who went about his life in a neat and organized way.

He began to explain where to find the cortisone creams, but then thought better of it. "You know what?" he said, glancing behind me and finding that no one else was waiting in line, "I'll just show you where they are. That'll be much easier." He came out from the counter and led me to the right aisle, pointing out the various brands of cream and the merits of each. I definitely didn't need such in-depth explanations, but I let him go on. I was in no hurry that morning. The grocery store was my only stop, the only place I was likely to see and interact with other people. I stood there nodding and smiling, secretly glad I had asked for his expertise, which he seemed to be all too ready to give. I watched his bright eyes, and wondered: how often do we go through life, not recognizing each other, not giving one another the chance to help when we can?

I usually speed through my day, pretending I have all the answers and buying into our culture's message about the primacy of the individual, so often forgetting our interconnected nature. And there would have been a time when I'd have been too anxious to be this vulnerable and ask for help for fear of "bothering" someone or causing them trouble. In this case, I would have missed out on a moment that I carried with me for hours and even days to come, sharing the incident with friends and students, especially my surprise and strange pleasure when the pharmacist lightly tapped my shoulder as we said goodbye like we'd known each other for years.

At Home in the Moment

We have to consciously study how to be tender with each other until it becomes a habit.

—Audre Lorde

Today, a Whole Foods cashier made me feel human again. When I pushed my cart into the nearest checkout line, just as I was about to load my items onto the conveyor, she came around the corner and said, "I can take you on Three. There's nobody there but me!"

She was a slightly older woman, hair pulled back in a ponytail, and she looked as tired as I felt. Yet she laughed wildly as I came over and said to her, "Thank you for finding me." We chatted a bit, and at the end she warned me that a bag of glass bottles was heavier than I might like. "I don't know how long of a day you've had," she said, grunting as she handed it over. "Long enough," I said, to which she replied: "Right?" I looked into her bright, weary eyes as if we'd both just stepped onto the same boat together. Then we said goodbye, and I told her to enjoy her night, for once meaning it with every fiber of my being.

Our whole interaction, when I think back on it, was a series of small kindnesses, little moments of tenderness and caretaking, like when she placed one of my reusable bags between a few glass bottles of kombucha so they wouldn't clink together and break. Or when she insisted on helping me bag my items, though I could easily have handled it. Even that one word just before the transaction was over—*Right?*—contained so much empathy that I felt more like myself, more human, than I had all day at work.

Over and over, I am reminded that this is all it takes to give one another the sense of belonging we lose so easily, especially in cities where efficiency and speed are prized above all else. It makes me think of what author and educator Parker Palmer said: "We must invite, not command, the soul to speak." We cannot force the deeper parts of ourselves to rise to the surface, but they can be invited by the choice to take care of ourselves, and by moments when someone gently coaxes the shy soul back out into the world. By the time I got back to my car, I couldn't stop smiling, and, suddenly, I didn't mind so much the hour-long drive home. Though she'll never know what she did for me, just as we can never know how much our kindness might change the life of another, that cashier gave me a home again in the moment.

The Voicemail

Some days have such blazingly bright moments at their center you know you'll hold onto that light for a long time to come. This afternoon, I called my mom to see if she needed to place her weekly grocery order online, reminding her that Christmas was just around the corner and the shoppers may be especially busy. She didn't seem too worried, but did thank me for the package of Reese's Peanut Butter Cups I sent her as part of the week of Christmas surprises I have planned this year.

"Finding that in the mail made me feel so good," my mother said.

I heard my grandmother chiming in from the background. "Me too!" she said.

I told her I was glad, having almost forgotten that I'd ordered it online a few days ago and marveling that something so small could lift them both up so much. In the past, I've had boxes of gourmet chocolates sent, baskets of assorted cookies, but I've found that their tastes run to the simple, and they prefer what they know.

After we got off the phone, I sat down at my laptop and ordered them some of the club sandwiches they rave about, from a place just down the road from the apartment they share. I'm old enough that it still boggles my mind, how I can sit nearly a thousand miles away in Vermont and arrange for meals to arrive at their doorstep in Arnold, Missouri, at the exact time I want them to, and can receive updates via text message about who delivered the meals and when. As I ordered their sandwiches just the way they like them, Brad leaned over and watched me, insisting that I also throw in two double chocolate chip cookies, even though I didn't think they needed the extra calories.

"It's Christmas!" he said. How could I argue with that?

He and I then bundled up and went on a long walk together, tracing the back roads to an old abandoned farmhouse we love to visit, with a view of Mount Equinox rising above it. As we walked in the white glare of winter sunshine, Brad kept pointing out puffs of snow that would cascade down from the loaded branches of trees, little silent explosions of glitter that lingered in the bone-chilling air.

"There it is again," he said, pointing, and we paused on the mostly empty road, watching the snowy explosions unfold in the light.

When we got home, I noticed the time and said, "Mom should have her sandwiches by now."

I looked at my phone and, sure enough, there were several texts from the delivery person and a voicemail waiting from my mom. I put my phone on speaker, and we both stood there at the counter listening.

"Do you know how great you are?" was my mother's first line. She said how perfect it was to find the sandwiches waiting in the bag by the door just as she began to wonder what they'd have for dinner. "You're the greatest," she said again, and then: "You're about the best thing that ever happened to me."

Brad and I were laughing at all the accolades—we both have loving mothers who think the world of us—and, I must admit, I was also tearing up. That a gesture so simple and easy—just a few clicks and a bit of typing—could bring this much gratitude and joy to two people I care about still seems incomprehensible to me.

"You have to save that message," Brad said. I told him "Of course" and emailed it to myself, knowing how many times I'd listen to it again in the future.

Savor This

I have been thinking a lot lately about all those rituals and chores I usually rush past as if they are of no consequence. It struck me this morning how often I bring a hint of resentment or even neutrality to what I'm doing, even though I could be finding deep pleasure in the task, knowing I'm offering a kindness to someone else, and to myself at the same time. I was rinsing out Brad's thermos for perhaps the thousandth time in our life together so far, which I fill with coffee or tea for him each morning. As I rubbed a sudsy sponge over the small cap and cup, and then around the rim of the thermos itself, and as I felt the hot water doing its work, it occurred to me how seldom I have brought a true gratitude to the many things I do for him. Aren't these chores also gifts I'd desperately miss if they were gone?

Pouring cream into his coffee and watching him finish a bowl of Raisin Bran before heading off to work at the farm, I remembered how it was just after my father died more than twenty years ago after his battle with hepatitis C. How often I'd resented driving him to doctors' appointments or fetching him just the right kind of orange juice he craved (Veryfine, in a glass bottle, if possible). He was too sick to do most things for himself, but being only twenty years old myself, I was too young to see that things would not go on like this forever. Some part of me always thought he would just get better, and we wouldn't have to wait on him like this anymore. One of my cousins took me aside at the time and tried to help me see the reality of our situation. "You know," Jimmy said, "Your dad could die at any time. He might only have a few months left." I thought my cousin was just being cruel and negative. I shrugged off his tough love and went on believing that my father could never leave us.

And just a few months later, when my dad did pass away just days before Christmas, the shock of it began to set in. He had always been able to fix anything and make us all feel safe. I just assumed he would somehow beat this disease, too, that he could fix himself, even though there wasn't a cure back then. I was devastated by the loss, but even more so because I had not appreciated all the little things I did for him, all the moments we shared together before he was gone. It was still too fresh all those years ago for me to bring words to my experience, but I did make a conscious promise to myself that this would never happen again, not if I could help it. I would be as present as possible in each moment with the people I love, relishing the time we had together. And, so, a gentle voice came to me today as I rinsed Brad's thermos, saying: Savor this daily task because you never know how many times you'll get to do it. I imagined Brad at the farm later on, seated at the sunstruck picnic table overlooking the pond, uncapping and pouring a cup of his steaming coffee, bringing it to his lips. How each sip would become a kiss we'd share over and over, a gift I get to offer him and myself every morning we wake, alive, together.

Feels Like Home

When Brad and I decided to get married, we agreed on a small ceremony here in our tiny Vermont village of Shaftsbury in an old church that now serves as a community center. I will never forget the kindness of Brad's mother, his sister Diane, cleaning up the building, sweeping all the floors and wiping down the windows, picking zinnias for the mason jars laid out on the tables, and organizing the potluck we had insisted on, preferring a celebration to a table full of gifts we didn't really need. It was a windswept and sun-drenched October day as we stood among layers of fallen leaves in the fields outside and said our own vows to each other, as my dear poet-friend Megan Buchanan married us, her son Avery ringing the church bells over and over.

I've never enjoyed large ceremonies or events. I didn't attend my graduations for college or graduate school for this very reason, preferring to stay out of the limelight. Yet, everything about this day felt right to me, simply meant to be. Brad and I had only been together for about a year before I got on my knees on a dusty dirt road in New Zealand and asked him to marry me. When we planned the wedding, we gave friends and family just a few weeks' notice before the date, which meant we all had to leap into action to make it happen. My so-called rational brain wondered if it was all too soon and kept me wide awake and panicky the night before, stricken with fear of the largest commitment I would ever make—even as I knew in my bones Brad was the right man for me. I even picked a fight that night when he came home from spending time with his buddies, angry (or so I thought) that he had left me at home all alone on such a special evening. I think he realized that my anxiety was taking over in that moment, and eventually forgave me.

When I woke up the next morning, as sunlight crested the mountains and pressed along the edges of the drawn shades, as our whole house brightened with the new day, it felt as if the fear was not quite gone, but right-sized—just a little dot of healthy apprehension that's natural in the face of growth and change.

I'll never forget the delectable carrot cake our friend Andrew baked for us, with carrots fresh from the farm where Brad works. Or the cake topper our friend Becca had found—the silhouette of two suited men holding hands, with "Mr. & Mr." written in cursive above them. I'll never forget all those homemade dishes steaming on the tables as our community came out to celebrate us, and that moment of looking around when it dawned on me that I was now a part of Brad's tight-knit family (his sister, Diane, and her husband, Jason, having driven all the way up from North Carolina just to help with our spur-of-the-moment marriage). I also saw that, in spite of all my moving around over the years, jumping from state to state and job to job, from one random apartment to another, I had finally settled down in a place that felt like home. I couldn't help but feel overwhelmed by that truth as I sat at one of the tables sipping my glass of sparkling apple cider and staring into all those joyful, welcoming faces. I thought back to that morning when we had gone to our Town Hall to fill out the paperwork for our marriage, and the town clerk, Marlene, had been so excited to help us, she could hardly contain herself. "My first marriage!" she said. Even now, when we come out to vote or attend a town meeting, Marlene rushes up with wide-open arms to hug us, sometimes even reminiscing that she was the one who helped to make our marriage official.

What a kind and wise thing we do for ourselves when we gather the courage to push against the usual patterns we know are unhealthy, and which we sometimes can't seem to resist falling into, because they are strangely comfortable, and so familiar. The dance of intimacy with Brad has not always been easy for either of us, and there were plenty of times when I just wanted to escape, when I felt too challenged to stay. During arguments, I would think about moving again, but some calmer voice rose up and told me how much I would regret it, even if it did feel like such a leap of faith to say yes to staying in one place with my person, putting down the tendrils of roots that only grow stronger and more resilient with time.

Giving What We Can

This morning, as I took my cup of strong coffee to the desk in my office, Brad said, "It's gonna be quite a sunrise," his way of reminding me to look up from my notebook now and then. He didn't want me to miss the pink streamers of clouds stretching out across the sky, seemingly lit from within. And when I saw that light show beginning outside in the cold, I said to myself: I can't believe I get to be alive for another sunrise, for one more day. As Maya Angelou once put it: "This is a wonderful day. I've never seen this one before!"

I had the same feeling last night as I lay in bed, rubbing the fine golden hairs on Brad's arm as he slipped off to sleep. I was staring up through the skylight again, one of my favorite pastimes, and could see all the constellations, all the starlight that works so hard to make its way toward us. I thought back to a time in my life when I didn't feel so grateful and remembered how I used to act so annoyed any time my dad asked for a massage before bed. I wasn't quite twenty years old then, and my father was dying, though none of us could really admit it. He had contracted hepatitis C back in his teens when he shared the same bottles of ink with some guys he knew as they drew homemade tattoos on their arms. The disease was now ravaging his body, causing discomfort, swelling, and slowly harming his liver. Though my dad was the sole provider in our family—my mother couldn't work because of her MS and agoraphobia—he eventually had to stop going to the plastics factory because of the pain.

I don't quite know how the nightly massages became our thing, but probably my dad had complained so much about his back and shoulder pain that I eventually offered to help. In truth, I couldn't do much else. He'd be lying in the bedroom across the bed on his stomach and call out to me, almost sheepish and afraid to ask when I came in. I'm ashamed to say that I sometimes rolled my eyes and sighed, not realizing the severity of his illness and how much fear he must have felt. I didn't realize my own power to bring a little relief to a man who had been a very good father—never afraid to cry or tell my brother and me that he loved us, always slow to anger. "Jay Jay," he would call out my nickname, short for James Junior, and I'd step reluctantly into the bedroom, already knowing what he wanted, but making him ask anyway. "Would you give me a massage?"

I don't think I ever refused, even if he asked just after I'd worked a long shift as a cashier at Target or spent all day in classes. I watched the digital clock on his nightstand as I worked the knots from his muscles, making a deal with myself: just another fifteen or twenty minutes, then I could stop.

Now, of course, I'd give anything to have those minutes back, offering what relief I could in his last months. Rubbing Brad's arm made me remember those times with my father when I took his health for granted. I took his unconditional love, and those intimate final moments we shared together for granted, too, and I never want to make the same mistake again. I know I still slip up and say the unkind thing or get exasperated with those I love, just as I did with Brad the night before our wedding. But losing my father at twenty years old, though it was the hardest thing I've ever had to face, has also been one of the greatest kindnesses I've received. His death taught me to savor every moment, to give compassion as often as I can, even when it feels like work at first. Feeling exhausted, annoyed, or resentful, we might think we have nothing left to offer someone else, but thinking back to all those times I gave my father a massage anyway, I'm grateful now that I dug deep and trusted that he wouldn't ask for help unless he really needed it. Imagine if we gave the people in our lives the benefit of the doubt, believing in their needs. I remember this, too: I always felt better afterward for offering what little I could, seeing peace fall across my father's stubbled face as he eased into sleep.

More Fully Human

At a café recently, I watched an older woman at the next table finish her cup of coffee. Every now and then, the cup would rattle as it met the saucer beneath, and her arm would begin to twitch and spasm, her legs suddenly restless under the table. I thought she must have Parkinson's disease, though she seemed at peace, beaming a smile to the crowded tables around her. She appeared nearly comfortable in that body that betrayed her. When she rose, half-walking, half-shuffling to the counter, holding up a few crumpled dollar bills, the young woman at the register visibly flinched. Her face darkened as the joking smile she'd been flashing to the rest of the customers vanished. "What can I do for you?" she said stiffly to the older woman, who had to point with difficulty to the pastry she wanted with a wildly trembling finger.

I don't blame that barista for turning so dark when she saw the other woman struggling. I've done the same thing. Yet, I had never witnessed so obvious an instance of someone armoring up against another person standing right there before her. Why do we guard ourselves against the suffering or pain of others? Are we afraid their difficulty will rub off on us, that they'll ask us to carry their burdens for them? Or is it because defects of the body, especially those illnesses associated with aging, cause us to face our own mortality head-on? More than anything else, I believe we react this way because we recognize that we are all a part of the same human family. We fear the pain we see in others because, deep down, we want to fix it, and know that we cannot.

I have felt this firsthand with both of my parents, who fell ill in their thirties, and it has been part of my journey to make peace with the fact that I could not save my father from the ravages of hepatitis C, and cannot cure my mother's multiple sclerosis, agoraphobia, or the breathing troubles she's now developed after years of smoking. Often, if we can't fix something, we want to turn away in hopelessness and despair, pretend the pain isn't there. Yet, a consistent and kind presence in the face of suffering is all that's required to make the leap from thinking only about ourselves to humbly holding space for the struggles of others. That's all they need from us. In moments of empathy, whether with a sick parent or even a stranger in a café, when we can see that all pain is one pain, we become more fully human, no longer afraid of the suffering of others.

Ordinary Repair

Lately, I have become a student of the ordinary, asking each moment: what are you here to teach me? This was especially true recently, as my mother entered the hospital for severe neck and back pain associated with her multiple sclerosis, then ended up having a heart attack while waiting to be seen in the ER. She spent a harrowing week in the hospital with cognitive difficulties, convinced that the phones were being tapped and that family members who called were being impersonated by hospital staff. I had never been so frightened for her well-being before. She was eventually released, and a urinary tract infection turned out to be the cause of her strange and paranoid behavior. But for weeks after, her brain remained foggy, and when we talked she would utter the same phrase over and over: "I'm just confused." During this difficult time, every day began for me with a rush of worry, especially since I live a thousand miles away and can do so little to help. And each night before bed, I would be so consumed with anxiety, it took me hours to fall asleep.

Most of us are no strangers to a life of persistent fear and worry, yet I was struck by just how much my own personal world had been built upon the foundation of my mother always being there in the tiny senior apartment she shares with my grandmother, filled with overstuffed chairs and the always-blaring TV. Once that stability was called into question, and we began to wonder if she could keep caring for herself and my grandmother, I felt my own life tilting toward uncertainty, as if I might never find solid ground again.

What saved me were reminders from friends, my therapist, and my husband to seek out moments of deep self-care, setting aside the time for myself that I didn't feel quite right taking, given that my mother was still suffering and so far away. Self-care had never been harder. I would take walks to the end of our road to check the mail, with the canopy of maples stretching overhead, making a green tunnel filled with dappled light that delighted me each time I passed beneath. But, by the time I got back home, my stomach had twisted up in knots again, as I realized how much emotion I was pushing under and not feeling, needing to let it all pass through me.

The other unexpected kindness of this time arrived as the ordinary chores I would normally have put off. One morning, I drove to the post office to mail some packages of books to friends. Often, envelopes will sit in my car for weeks before I make the time for this task, but that day, I relished the feel of the smooth brown envelopes in my hands before I sent them off. I felt amused by the little brass key I used to unlock my P.O. box, pulling out a rolled-up newspaper and a card with a watercolor on the front that my friend Anne had painted herself. Her colorful poppies lifted my spirits, and there was something about the physicality of everything that seemed so alive to me in those "in-between moments" of not caring for or worrying about anyone else, just doing what needed to be done.

When I got back to the car, I knew I couldn't go home yet. I drove instead to a nearby nature preserve with the windows rolled all the way down and parked beside the hedgerow. Just sitting there with the warm air passing through, soaking in the trilling calls of a song sparrow hidden in the honeysuckle, healed something for me. I felt like a fish briefly released back into familiar water, my body no longer having to work so hard to breathe as I eased back into the flow of life, resisting nothing. I began to see my fear and anxiety for what they are, the result of a deep empathy, of letting my heart break for my mother and her situation, and for my own helplessness in the face of her loneliness and pain. That raw openness to love made me more present than I'd been in months, possibly even years. I saw each person I encountered as whole and lovely, each object I touched as shimmering and holy, remembering how quickly our circumstances can change on this earth.

I thought of the Jewish concept of *tikkun olam,* which translates as "repair of the world." This often refers to acts of kindness performed to help others, but, traditionally, the concept was also connected to the notion that our task as humans is to find the light hidden in every event and every fellow person. No matter how painful or plain the moment, we can always seek out some kernel of light that will help us find our way. Keeping that knowledge close, I made it a practice to welcome the everyday chores and interactions as evidence of my aliveness—from filling the tank with gas and grocery shopping, to meeting with the town assessor about the value of our property and home. Even that half hour seated in an old desk chair in the town office, talking about square footage and foundations, became precious to me because I knew once again, as if for the first time, there would never be another day like this one.

Be Kind to Yourself

This morning, I left Brad still stretching on his yoga mat. As I knelt down to kiss him goodbye, he said something he's never said to me before: "Be kind to yourself." The words caught me off guard, but didn't return to me until later, when I was taking a walk through the woods, noticing the yellow leaves of poplars spilling out on the path near our house, and thinking: I get to experience another autumn in one of my favorite places on the planet. I realized then that I was unconsciously doing just what he'd encouraged me to do, taking a walk in the middle of the day when there was still plenty of work to keep me occupied and groceries to pick up. I'd also brought a large mug of green tea with me, an extra spoonful of honey swirled in. And I ended my walk early when I started to feel hungry, instead of pushing onward, even pausing on the trail for a few seconds to take in the rustling leaves of the changing maples, to watch a robin flit off between light-dappled branches.

Having someone else give me permission to be kind to myself made it that much easier to follow through. For years, I thought that if Brad was at work, I needed to stay busy too, and not just with my creative work. I would force myself to do unpleasant chores around the house or run errands in order to feel better about how I'd spent my time—in order to feel *worthy* of that free time in the first place. I filled my days with tasks I thought I *should* be doing, instead of listening deeply to what I needed, or finding ways to cherish the simple tasks that make up our lives. How often do we turn away from self-love because we believe we don't deserve it, haven't done enough to earn it? Now, I'm trying to be more indulgent with myself, knowing that a slow walk or an afternoon meditation can actually make me more peaceful and available to everyone else in my life. In these anxious times, we can't underestimate the power of self-compassion to turn us into the helpers we'd all like to become, giving what we can to others from a full inner well.

Recharge Yourself

I've been doing an almost daily walk in a local nature preserve for the past several months now, and typically I come away with insights about my life, both large and small. Today, I kept thinking about how hard it is for me to do nothing, to just sit still and *be* without any expectation of outcome or productivity. For someone who enjoys meditation, you'd think I would be better at doing nothing, yet that practice (for me at least) has a purpose behind it, even if that intention is simply to pay loose attention to my breath and watch the thoughts as they filter through my mind. I've wondered for years why I have this constant need to feel I'm not only being productive, but am also fulfilling my larger purpose on the planet—a sure recipe for self-criticism and pressure. This morning, it finally hit me on my walk: In many ways, neither of my parents ever lived out their full lives or were able to realize their dreams. As Carl Jung once said: "Nothing affects the life of a child so much as the unlived life of its parent."

My father died at the age of forty-three from hepatitis C—the same age I am right now. In his last years, I watched him wither and fade, able to do less and less, until paramedics had to carry him out of the house on a stretcher that final time. As I often say, his death has been one of the hardest things I've ever endured, yet at the same time, it's become one of my greatest gifts too, because the loss has proven to me how singularly precious every moment of life really can be. My father showed us all how, even at the end of his life, not to give in to fear.

Just weeks before he passed away, he gathered my mother, brother, and me in the living room where he lay on the pullout couch, surrounded by his beloved deer heads mounted on the walls above him. He said, "I don't want you all to be sad when I go. Because I know what's coming, and I'm ready." I still remember the way we all looked at each other with stricken eyes and told my dad not to be so negative. But he had made his peace with death, and twenty years later, I see that conversation as the ultimate kindness because, in hindsight, it gives me great comfort to know that he was fully aware of what he was facing—even if we were not.

Losing him so early, of course, it makes sense that I would go into overdrive in my own life, trying to accomplish as much as possible, given the motivating knowledge that this could all end at any time. As my mother's life illustrates, there are other ways for our life to end, even while we're still alive. After the birth of my brother in her early twenties, she developed a debilitating case of agoraphobia, which kept her from driving a car, holding a job, or going to crowded places like malls and grocery stores. Then, in her thirties, she was diagnosed with multiple sclerosis, making it difficult for her to move around or to trust her body enough to do simple things like standing on a stool to change a light bulb or go up and down stairs. Now, my mother also suffers from COPD and must be hooked up to an oxygen machine for twenty-four hours a day, which means she seldom leaves the house. I'm grateful she remains able to walk with the help of a cane or walker and can still do simple chores, like cook meals for herself and my grandmother, who shares an apartment with her. Yet when we talk, she often laments all the things she couldn't do for my brother and me while growing up—bringing baked treats to our classes at school for holidays, going with us on field trips, picking us up from after-school activities, which we mostly had to avoid because we had no way of getting home. "I always wanted to do more," she says.

It is no surprise then that I have tried to live my life so that I would never have to say that, so I wouldn't carry the same regrets at the end. Fear is a powerful driver, and now I see how much it has pushed me to achieve, sometimes to the detriment of my own joy, often keeping me from the playfulness that renews the spirit. I've had much more free time on my hands lately now that I no longer commute to a job more than an hour away, but I've still struggled to accept the time and space as a gift.

Today, however, as I wandered the trails of the park, kicking through an orange-and-red carpet of fallen leaves, with a chill October wind tossing my hair, I heard these words in my mind: *I'm giving you this time to recharge yourself.* I can't say where the voice came from, but it brought instant calm and relief. In the past, during periods of low activity, instead of sinking into that freedom, I'd become afraid once again that I wasn't doing enough, and then would start adding more and more to my schedule until I felt drained and overwhelmed. Now, I say to myself: What if you just embrace this space as exactly what you need? Even if you feel bored. Even if you worry you've lost your sense of purpose. Even if it forces you to be more creative about how you choose to fill your time. What if you had faith in the changing seasons of life, knowing there's a time and place for activity and growth, and a time and place for the hibernation and quiet that will allow you to emerge rested and restored on the other side?

KiNDNESS PRACTiCE
THE HABIT OF SELF-CARE

Self-care is one of the most potent forms of kindness because it keeps us available to ourselves and to the other people in our lives. But self-care is not just about candles, bubble baths, and special lotions, as our culture might sometimes have us believe. It's not just about treating ourselves to tangible rewards when we feel down, though this can be helpful at times. We practice true kindness toward ourselves when we take the time to create new and nourishing habits, when we work to ensure that this type of self-compassion becomes a regular part of our daily routine.

I remember when I used to teach at a university in the city more than an hour from my house. I would often arrive rattled from the long drive or frustrated from sitting in traffic, and I found that this rushed energy followed me into the classroom. After weeks of struggling, I began to leave the house a little earlier in the mornings, allowing room for a traffic jam, or for a few extra minutes of sitting in the parking lot and sipping my coffee, watching squirrels frolic in the spindly trees as sleepy students locked up their cars, bent over from the weight of their backpacks. This space for "soul time," as I like to call it, became a ritual, and eventually seeped into other areas of my life. When I'd come home, for instance, after that endless commute, carrying that same rattled energy, I started giving myself permission to walk in the fields around our home, feeling the sunshine on my skin, even sometimes sitting among the goldenrod and Queen Anne's lace, feeling healed by nature again. At first, I didn't consciously call these practices kindness or self-care, but once I was able to name them and see the peace these habits brought to my life, they became even easier to integrate into each day. Even when I felt pressed for time, I knew that I deserved these little joys, and I noticed that they made me much more attentive to my husband and loved ones, as well as to my students. It became more automatic to say a resounding "yes" to my own needs.

Invitation for Writing & Reflection

As you move more deeply into the daily practice of compassion, how might you integrate more self-care into your life? Sit down and make a list of the ways you've recently taken care of yourself, seeing this, too, as a necessary form of kindness, especially in difficult times.

The Blue Blanket

It was a few nights before the twentieth anniversary of my father's death, and I was thinking of the fragility of life. This struck me as we got ready for bed, and I told Brad I would watch over the fire in the woodstove so he could go to sleep. He settled in on the couch, where he still spends most of his nights. It's been three weeks since the surgery to remove his wisdom teeth, and he still can't lie flat, still has to get up multiple times to take ibuprofen and use ice packs on his cheeks.

"Where's the blue blanket?" he asked, an almost childlike lilt to his voice. He meant the dark-blue fleece blanket we often keep on the couch, which he uses in addition to his wool blanket to stay warm at night.

"It's in the reading nook," I said. "I'll bring it over before I go upstairs."

Brad slipped off to sleep almost immediately, and as I lay there next to the stove—flames rolling upward inside, bright yellow and blue—I thought about those few months before we lost my father. How every little thing became so important to him. One time, I brought him a bowl of his usual low-sodium chicken soup with buttery Ritz Crackers for lunch and laid it all out on the TV tray in front of him. He looked down at the spoon resting on a folded-up paper napkin.

"That's the wrong one," he said with a wide, indulgent smile, as if I might have been trying to pull one over on him. "You know I like the good spoons."

He meant the newer, green-handled set of silverware in the drawer. Shaking my head and cursing under my breath at the nerve of his request, I went to fetch the so-called "correct" spoon. Yet, had I known I would lose him just a few weeks after that, I never would have gotten so frustrated. I would have understood that every small pleasure was essential, because some part of him already knew that each day could be his last. This was why, although his doctors forbade all salt because his body had swollen with excess water and his liver and kidneys no longer functioned properly, all he craved was salt. I did the grocery shopping, and because I wanted and needed him to stay healthy, I followed his diet to the letter, filling the cart with turkey burgers and shredded wheat cereal. Food was always central to him, though, and whenever summer came around, he'd drive to the nearest farm stand and buy a bag bursting with homegrown tomatoes. He couldn't wait to slice into that first juicy beefsteak, spread salt on it, and feast.

It should have come as no surprise to us then that, after he passed, we found his stash—jars of dill pickles hidden in the hall closet and a canister of Morton Salt he kept in the cabinet of his nightstand. We found Big Mac wrappers stuffed under the car seats and a few slices of his favorite lunch meat, called Krakow, from Pietukowski's, the Polish deli he must have sneaked off to in the city. My mom, brother, and I couldn't help but laugh with tears in our eyes as we uncovered all the evidence of his indulgences in spite of our own best intentions. But I also felt the grind of guilt, wishing I hadn't denied him those final pleasures during what ended up being the end of his life. Why couldn't I have been less rigid and recognized that life *is* the small things, the little moments we don't believe will add up to much.

Twenty years is a long time to live without someone you loved so deeply, yet his final months remain so vivid in my mind; it was as if I could have slipped into any one of those days as I lay on the floor by the flickering fire. In some strange way, I feel as if life gave me another chance when I met Brad, to love a man fiercely again without fearing I'd be abandoned, and, at the same time, embracing the fact that our time together will always be limited, even if we're alive together another forty years. This is the beauty of all life—that it is temporary, that every moment is given to us just once, and it is up to us how we receive it. Do we relish our time, cultivating gratitude for the messiness and joy? Do we recognize the importance of so-called small kindnesses, like the green-handled spoon or the blue fleece blanket, and indulge the ones we love the most? Or do we wait for some catastrophe or illness to shake us from our daily sleep?

I don't live every day with the gratefulness and generosity I know I am capable of. There are plenty of times when I'm so tired or depressed that I think: what does it matter? But then I'll remember my father, how none of us thought it was possible that he'd be gone at the age of forty-three. Then I know that every passing moment contains a choice, and if we can gently hold this truth close to our chests—without overwhelming ourselves with too much pressure or fear—we'll see how much it all matters, just as I did tonight, spreading the blue blanket over the man I love as he lay deep in sleep.

Delivery

We saw the pair of headlights in our driveway cutting through the already-thick darkness of five o'clock and then a figure getting out of the car and opening the gate I had just walked down to close a few minutes ago.

"Who is that?" Brad asked, getting on his coat and boots as I scrutinized the car now heading for our house to see if I recognized it. I left my carrots sizzling on the stove, slipped on my sandals, and stepped out onto the packed snow of the driveway, curious to see who this might be.

The car backed up onto our hill, and the driver's side window rolled down to reveal the ruddy face of our friend Melissa. She and her husband, Greg, an old friend of Brad's from high school, run our favorite café in town, where she makes all the delicious quiches, scones, and pies. As we exchanged our chilly greetings, she handed over a package from the passenger seat.

"I made a ton of cookies and tarts," she said, "so I thought I'd share."

We talked for a while about her young son's upcoming surgery, how worried they were, and made plans to get together after his procedure at the end of the month.

"If you need anything," Brad said, referring to Gavin's surgery, "just let us know." I think we both knew there was not much we could do for this little family, but I watched Melissa's face visibly relax as she received the gift of those words from Brad, knowing that we meant it.

It had been an off-kilter day for me, as I showed up on the wrong day for a doctor's appointment and then shopped for groceries, forgetting half of what we needed and buying too many of the random items—sweet potato chips and gluten-free brownie bites—that I toss in the cart when I'm hungry and tired. All day, I had felt like curling up in a cave and sleeping through the new year with instructions to wake me when everything in our country and the world has finally gotten better. Yet, as I stood out in the cold wearing only my sandals and a thin, long-sleeve shirt, hoping my carrots weren't burning on the stove, I felt some of the frustration from the day lifting, floating away with the bits of snow the wind kept sweeping up around us.

We finally said goodbye, I rushed in to my carrots, and as I prepared the rest of our stir-fry, I felt myself welling up at the sheer kindness of Melissa's gesture. It was made even more special by the fact that she didn't just stuff the cookie tin into our mailbox, but, instead, insisted on driving all the way down our twisting driveway to hand it off in person, perhaps sensing the necessity of the exchange, how much we needed to see a friendly face and remember that people care, especially as I bit into one of her chewy peppermint cocoa cookies and closed my eyes to appreciate every rich bite.

White Chicken Chili

When my father first got sick, my family and I were in and out of hospitals, trying to keep him as healthy as possible. During one of his longer stays at St. Anthony's, even though I was holding down a part-time job at Target and attending college full-time, I made sure to be there every day I could for him. None of us wanted to believe he was so close to the end, but we all must have sensed it.

This time in the hospital, things had turned even more serious. He'd lapsed into a coma from which he almost didn't emerge. When he finally did wake up, he seemed at first to hallucinate as we all kept vigil in his room, standing around the bed. At one point, he lifted his hands and gestured in the air. "Piles of cigarettes," he said. "Piles and piles." A slight smile formed on his face. He had just quit smoking a few months before, so I thought maybe he was still craving the nicotine. Eventually, he somehow came out of it all, defying the dire predictions of doctors who'd encouraged us to call all our family members and say our final goodbyes. Our time together now felt like a gift, and as I sat at his bedside, amazed at the clarity that had returned to his blue eyes, I gripped the wide, callused hand that had once fixed everything for us. I decided not to waste another second of our time together.

Yet, whenever I stepped into the bathroom in the ICU and glanced in the mirror at myself, or looked around at my brother, my mom, and my grandmother, I saw the exhaustion in our dark-ringed and red-rimmed eyes. One day, I began walking the mazelike corridors just for exercise and stumbled on a little café in a faraway wing of the hospital. I glanced up at the menu and found an eclectic mix of items, including cornbread and white chicken chili. It felt like such an indulgence, since I knew my father still lay suffering in his bed, but I couldn't help myself: I ordered a bowl of that white chili, curious to try something I'd never had before. It was unlike me to exclude my family, and as I sat there in a booth with the steaming bowl in front of me, I felt afraid that someone would come along and see me taking this much-needed break for self-care, having realized how deeply and desperately hungry I was—not just for food, but also for time to myself to process what was happening with my dad.

Each spoonful of that spicy chicken chili was more delicious than the last—the chopped jalapeños waking my senses and the solitude giving me the strength to keep going another day. Sitting there alone felt like taking a stand for my own well-being, which, of course, had been suffering those past weeks and months as my dad's hepatitis C worsened. He would stay in the hospital for another week, and, every day I could, I made my way to the tiny café where I was convinced the cook made all the food herself from scratch, from her own recipes; it was just that good. Once or twice, I brought my family with me, but otherwise, I looked forward to that chili as a treat just for me, paying deep attention to every bite, trying to notice every flavor and spice.

In the midst of caretaking others, we easily sweep aside our own needs. We forget the simple pleasure of doing something ordinary, whether taking a walk, reading a book, or having a meal by ourselves. It can feel like a sacred act, this pause in which we recharge, when the attention paid to the loved one who's in pain is transferred to ourselves for a short while. It can feel like going to church, performing even the simplest chores, or running errands that might have seemed boring before, if we allow ourselves to soak up the dailiness of a world that goes on despite our personal worries, and the difficulties or losses we might face. I thought of my trips to the café as a little selfish at the time, and kept them a secret from my family. Yet, I needed a break, some slice of time that was my own to remember that I too was a human with needs. And, after each slow meal, I returned to my father's room in the ICU at least a bit more rested and ready to keep taking care of him for as long as I could.

One Last Time

Over twenty years ago, we left my father in the ICU where we had brought him because he was showing signs of pneumonia. He could still speak, and his mind was all there, but we'd had to call an ambulance to help us get him out of the house, to lift him out on a stretcher, through the front door and down the porch steps, because he could not get up off of the pullout sofa where he now spent most of his nights.

At the hospital, they set him up with an IV, and he seemed content in bed, propped up by a few fluffy pillows, his tray nearby with a cup of water and a straw. A nurse had just come in to tell us that visiting hours were over, and we might as well go home, get some sleep, and come back the next morning. My mother, my brother, Ron, and I stood huddled around the bed, unwilling to leave him just yet. My mother leaned toward him, smoothing a few of my father's stray white hairs from his forehead.

"You think you'll be alright?" she asked. He waved away her worries.

"I'll be fine," he said, then looked at Ron and me. "Hey, before you go, would you two get me a bottle of soda from the machine out there? Make sure it's *really* cold."

I smiled a little to myself, thinking that we have no control over the temperature of the sodas in the machine, but I told him we'd be right back.

When my brother and I returned, my mom said the nurse had come in again and told us it really was time to go.

"I don't like leaving him like this," she said. "I can't stand it."

"We'll be back early in the morning," I assured her, feeling exhausted from the stress of the day and ready to curl up in my own bed.

Ron twisted open the soda, leaving it on the tray as we gathered up our things. "Are you sure you're gonna be okay?" my mom asked again. "I could sleep in this chair here."

"No, no, no. Go home and rest. I love you guys," my dad said. He lifted the bendable straw out of his cup of water. My mother and brother were making their way through the curtain. "Hey, Jay Jay," my dad said to me. "Would you move that Coke a little closer?"

I inched the cold bottle closer toward him on the plastic tray, and he stuck the straw inside. "Perfect," he said.

"Love you," I said.

"I love you, too," he said, nodding, already intent on taking a sip of the soda the nurses would never have allowed him to have.

And with those last words exchanged between us, the last words my father ever spoke to any of us—we left him alone in the ICU. When my mother called the next morning, we were told that he had slipped into a coma overnight, and that we should all get there as soon as we could to say our goodbyes. My mother turned frantic on the phone, asking why no one had called us that night, worried he was neglected and ignored. There wasn't much time to wonder, though, as we called up the rest of our family to gather at the hospital. We were told by the doctor that my father only had a matter of hours to live and was no longer able to breathe on his own.

I remember the chaos of that day spent in and out of waiting rooms, how the pain and confusion of what was happening became the center of our lives. Because it was what my father had wanted, he was eventually removed from the ventilator, and we waited for him to breathe his final breaths. It would take hours, and at one point in our vigil, I decided to go grab some food at a nearby diner with a friend, a hamburger and plate of fries that I barely touched, really just needing a break from the hospital.

I came back to the car on that cold December night watching flurries fly, and as I got inside, began to shiver uncontrollably. I knew I was probably in shock but couldn't stop what was happening until I breathed deeply, in and out, for a few minutes, managing to bring myself back from the brink of a panic attack. By the time I arrived in the ICU again and stepped into his crowded room, I knew he was gone.

"Come kiss your dad goodbye," my mom said to me through her tears, and I walked slowly to where he lay, and pressed my lips to the cool skin of his forehead.

I have heard stories that when people are dying, they will sometimes wait until certain family members are out of the room so they don't have to watch them take those last, difficult breaths. Of course, I can't say if this is what happened with my father, though I have often wondered why on earth I chose to leave his bedside when I knew he was likely to pass on so soon. Over the years, I have had to work hard to forgive myself for taking that break, coming to see that it was not selfish of me to step away and take the time I needed. I would also find out later that at the approximate moment I got into the car and began to shiver as I never had before, my father officially stopped breathing. My body must have known long before I did.

I have relived those few days again and again in the decades since he's been gone, as if to make sense of them, still trying to allow the pain to pass through me, knowing that grief never really goes away, but only changes over time.

I'll never forget the moment that I stepped out of the curtained room after kissing him goodbye, into the blinding light of the hallway again. A doctor wearing glasses and speaking with an Irish accent came up to me, just me, as if he had been sent by someone.

"I know this must be a shock for you," he said, placing a gentle hand on my arm. "I'm here if you'd like to talk about this."

"He was sick for a long time," I said with the detachment it would take me many years to move beyond. "It wasn't really much of a surprise."

"Still," the Irish doctor said, insisting. "It must be very painful."

I nodded and thanked him, then walked away to find the rest of my family drinking coffee from Styrofoam cups in one of the grieving rooms decorated with outdated pastel and gray wallpaper. Looking back, I'm grateful for that Irish doctor's unexpected kindness, inviting me to talk through and feel something I just wasn't ready to feel. I often wonder how my life might have turned out differently if I had taken him up on his invitation and said, "Yes, I would like to talk to someone," *anyone* about what I was now facing. I wish I could have admitted: the man who could always fix anything, who was the center of our whole family, is now gone, and I don't know what to do.

But everyone's grief is a journey they take on their own and at their own pace, stumbling and falling down on the path along the way. Over the years, I feel more and more grateful for all that my father's death has taught me, for the ways it's shown me how to live a kinder, more present life. I think often of his final request for the bottle of soda, how the last moment we shared was an act of love, as I moved that cold Coke just a little closer so he could reach it.

Go Slow

Let us slow down enough to truly notice all that is presenting itself
to us as a blessing.

—Kristi Nelson

At the library the other day, I overheard an elderly man and staff member talking about the record-breaking snow we had just received. The older man comes almost every day and sits at the same table near the windows, where he does his crossword puzzles. He walks with a shuffling gait and seems to be in pain, but is unfailingly polite to everyone. Many of the staff have adopted him and ask after his life, look out for him. As I listened in, the two men spoke of the difficulties of digging out from two feet of snow and moving through it. "You just have to go slow," the younger man said, staring out the windows at all the white. "Remember to take it slow," he repeated several times to the older man as he limped out of the building, driving home his point. And though those kind words were not meant for me, I took them to heart. Any reminder to move more slowly through our bustling lives comes as a benediction, an invitation to pause and pay attention to every step we take.

I had just recovered from a nasty, humbling cold and had to admit it was my own fault. I'd been rushing from place to place the week before, heart racing, always reaching forward to the next supposedly essential task or errand without staying present to the needs of my body, not noticing when I was worn out. I know that going slow, stepping into what I call "soul time," is the only natural pace for me. Yet, I convince myself—and our culture often assures me—that I must move as fast as I can to cross off all those things on my never-ending to-do list.

We are bound to forget this message, so we must repeat it to ourselves and each other like the small blessing it is: *Go slow.* Remember that you can enjoy almost anything if you give yourself the space and permission to appreciate it—the give of slushy snow beneath the boots, icicles hanging like stalactites from power lines, or the violent streamers of clouds lit up red during a winter sunset. I know that I can take a deep, clean breath of near-zero air and let it enliven me. Or I can rush to get inside out of the bitter cold and keep resisting what is real until my body finds a way to slow me down, until I notice again that the world is always longing for our loving attention.

Soul Time

You learn to go at your own pace because, if you don't, there's a backlash.
—Pema Chödrön

On our walk this morning, Brad sped ahead on the gravel road, needing to go at his own natural, much faster clip. This used to bother us both, but now we accept there will be some days when he's able to slow down and some days when I'm able to speed up. We've learned to give each other the space we need to be ourselves and move at our own pace through life.

I am a slower person by nature. I believe this is true for many people, yet our culture of achievement pushes us toward deadlines based on clock time, instead of soul time. Our souls know we are here to take joy in small things through careful attention and love and that we are never nourished by speed; in fact, more often than not, we must take the time to recover from pushing ourselves to move at a faster pace than we feel accustomed to. If we don't see what we see and feel what we feel in the moment, we reduce our chances of seeing and feeling it later, and thus living a truly connected life. We find kindness and love, after all, only in those gaps between tasks, and especially when we can take the time to relish whatever we're doing with our whole selves.

The truth of my own slowness didn't dawn on me until the day I was making guacamole for my friend Adrienne just before a dinner party. As I peeled and sliced each avocado, then diced a nice-sized shallot and mashed it all together in a bowl with salt and fresh-squeezed lemon juice, before adding the carefully chopped jalapeños, cilantro, and tomatoes, I told Adrienne I was sorry it was taking so long.

"I'm usually much faster," I said, shaking my head.

"Honey," Adrienne said, placing her hand on my back, "you don't do *anything* fast."

Her words stung at first, and I felt insulted. Soon I realized that, of course, it was true, and I could actually choose to take it as a compliment—which I finally did. I have always preferred walking where I need to go as opposed to driving, and driving to flying, and chopping by hand as opposed to using a blender. In fact, if it takes longer, I will most likely enjoy it more. As I thought about how my calling as a writer has also slowed me down over the years, I saw how much simpler and clearer my life could have been up to that point if I'd just accepted the truth of my natural slowness, instead of pushing myself to match the speed of others.

We can be productive even while taking our time. We can budget extra hours in our packed schedules for play, and resist filling what could be soul time in our days by letting our devices absorb so much of our attention. We can arrive at the airport early and offer others relief by letting them go ahead of us through security, or if a clerk apologizes for a long wait in a crowded store, we can tell them not to worry, that we are in no hurry. The Japanese have a word for this practice—*yutori*, which means intentionally building space in your life for the sole purpose of pleasure and enjoyment. Show up early for a meeting and sit in the car just listening and watching, or sit at a table alone in a café, instead of taking your coffee to go, and sip it slowly, noticing the customers rushing in and out, browsing the newspaper someone left behind. You may not move as slowly as I do, but all of our souls crave the time and space to enjoy the moments we're given.

Thanks for Doing That

At a meeting years ago, I made myself more vulnerable by sharing with colleagues that I would be spending the holidays taking care of my mother as she recovered from hernia surgery. I felt the need to bring humanity and reality to the proceedings, to acknowledge that we all have lives outside of our often all-consuming work. When the meeting ended, none of my fellow teachers commented on what I had said except my friend Shari. She stopped me in the hallway and said in a voice filled with compassion, "I hope your mom feels better." "I do too," I said, confessing that I would be staying with her for several weeks after the surgery. Shari took a deep breath and looked me in the eyes, "Thanks for doing that," she said.

I headed to my office, left speechless by her words that had, like a hot knife, cut through the day's formality. That's what a sudden kindness always does: it brings us closer to ourselves and draws us toward each other at the same time. I was moved by her expression of what I have come to think of as radical gratitude—thanking me for doing something that seemed to have nothing to do with her or her life.

Thanks for doing that. Her words have stayed with me because they remind me that any time we help someone else—no matter how small the gesture, even if we're doing our job or fulfilling some responsibility—we also help repair the world. The ripples of just one kind act extend out to those in our lives and to people everywhere, until everyone on the planet is touched by some trace amount of that original kindness. Any selfless act is a kind of love we carry with us everywhere we go—life's only real currency—and we can keep passing it on, paying it forward. This is not to say that we should always lay our own needs aside. Each of us should be thanked profusely when we take care of ourselves, too, since this sends ripples of light out into the world as well and leaves us more able to show up for others.

But why not express a radical gratitude, even if it doesn't seem to directly affect us? Why not thank the mother looking after her children, the bus driver, the letter carrier, the man who pushes open the train doors so a few more people can board at rush hour? Why not spend our lives looking for ways to help and watching for other helpers to recklessly thank for every selfless act they perform?

Helpers

Look for the helpers. You will always find people who are helping.

—Fred Rogers

Volunteers fanned out on the park trails that morning, picking up other people's litter, their hands wrapped in blue latex gloves. I sometimes carry a plastic bag with me when I go for a long walk along the dirt roads my husband and I love, and I gather up the tossed-out bottles, soda cans, and cigarette packs that dot the grass. But, more often than not, I forget, or lose heart and think it useless to clean up the trails and streets when the litter will just appear again tomorrow. I want to blame others for the carelessness we have all shown more than once in our lives.

Yet, something about seeing those groups of women and men spreading out across the park, even in the hundred-degree heat, gave me a much-needed jolt of joy. Here they were, doing a good deed without the promise of an immediate return and knowing full well they'd be back doing the same thing next month. They had given up their morning and were stuffing trash into bags so people like me could walk the trails, seeing nothing but the tall native grasses and joe-pye weed waving in the wind—nothing else to mar the natural beauty of the scene.

We get the idea that our actions need to be reciprocal, that if we do something unpleasant or difficult, the world owes us some reward in return. We often think: *what's in it for me?* But this is not how the world works. In my experience, anything worth doing—prayer, meditation, art-making, writing, exercise, volunteering—seldom brings immediate, tangible results beyond a brief, but not insignificant, feeling of greater connection. We have to take a leap and trust that what we do now, in every moment, will somehow affect not only ourselves, but also others in the future. If we've done the right thing, and then the next right thing, and checked in with our intentions, our actions will make positive ripples that others are bound to feel.

A colleague once told me that he refused to help his neighbor move out of the apartment next door because she had been annoying and noisy. Most of us have done the same thing, having withheld help or advice as payback, but we are the ones who feel most deprived after holding back. It makes us feel good to do something selfless, without expectation of reward or outcome, as long as we have the space and feel moved to give. It is easy to turn away from the litter in our yard, to say that we didn't put it there and won't pick it up, but part of the practice is to give up the idea of blame, and to keep doing those things that take care of ourselves and, thus, the whole world.

Heart-Shaped Bandage

My crown is in my heart, not on my head.

—William Shakespeare

I remember a few years ago when the doctors finally let me see my mother after her hernia surgery. She looked awful. It was good to see her after so many hours of worry—Did something go wrong? Will the surgery work? Will it make her pain worse? She had an oversized oxygen mask strapped to her face that muffled the words she was able to utter. She also still had a thick plastic tube running up her nose, which she kept tugging at and cursing, even as she told me how happy she was to see me, how little pain she felt now.

After hours alone in the waiting room, I felt jumpy and clenched with tension, yet I tried to be simply present at her bedside, to breathe out each worry into the antiseptic air. I rubbed her bare arms, the skin so dry there, and smoothed back the loose hairs from her forehead. Often, when I am caught in my own "emergency mode," when every new development seems a cause for panic, I forget to call on the universe for help. I forget that all pain is shared pain, that we are never completely alone with it. When things seem hopeless, I can forget that the key to unlocking our faith again is tenderness and gratitude for what is.

So, while I softly touched my mother's face and arms, I said *thank you* that she had made it through another difficult surgery, *thank you* for the time off from work that allowed me to be there with her and that would let me care for her for the next two weeks. *Thank you* for the loving mother who lay before me, who has never withheld a kind word or gesture and still calls her middle-aged son her baby. When I looked down at her hand, where the nurse had tried and failed to find a vein for the IV earlier, I said *thank you* for that lump of gauze taped there in the accidental shape of a heart.

I chose to take that bandage as a not-so-subtle reminder to live in the heart, to bring love and breathe space into even the most uncertain situations. Though my mother would fully recover after the surgery, I had no way of knowing that then. All I could do was mouth my silent gratitude and rub the dry skin of her hands, letting her know I was there.

Neighbors

My mother's voice on the phone sounded far away and faint, her throat scratchy as we spoke. She'd just spent several weeks in the hospital recovering from surgery. I had stayed with her a few weeks back and had just gotten home myself from several trips for work. I knew I needed rest, yet still felt guilty for not being there with her as she found her strength again.

Often, our conversations revolve around logistics—ordering groceries, helping her fill out certain insurance forms, connecting her with the wonderful folks at Meals on Wheels. But that Saturday, as I washed some lettuce and carrots for a salad, I decided to call and check in with her, see how she was doing.

"You called just to check in on *me*?" my mother said in her weak voice, clearly pleased that I had no other agenda.

She told me about the antibiotics she was taking and a mix-up with the pharmacy that meant two prescriptions were delivered instead of just one, giving me a rundown of her day. Then she began to describe how the upstairs neighbors were now helping to look after her. In the past, she's never been friendly with the other people who live in her building. She had been raised by my grandmother never to ask for help and to be distrustful of people who might offer it. My mother told me once recently about how a neighbor had knocked on her door with a tin of cookies several days in a row.

"You sure are making a habit of this," she said to this generous woman.

"Mom!" I said after she relayed the story. "Just be grateful in the future. It sounds like you're turning away her gift."

Perhaps the shift that's happened in the past few months is that she now knows she needs the interaction and help from other people.

"Sandra, that woman from upstairs, stopped by earlier," she said to me now. "She's gonna make a spaghetti dinner and asked me if I'd like to join her."

"That's really sweet," I said, noting the skepticism in her voice.

"Yeah, I told her she doesn't have to do that. I've got food in the fridge, but she said she wants to do it. She and that other lady upstairs, Gloria, have been picking up little things for me, too—some butter, and they're supposed to bring me a pack of toilet paper later."

I imagined my mother inching toward her apartment door whenever one of these women knocked, trailing the clear plastic tubes from her oxygen machine, which has to run day and night. I saw her face lighting up to see these strangers who have slowly become neighbors and friends to her. Though I've never met them, I could also see their smiling faces, their kind eyes. I felt a rush of gratitude that they would sense how much it means to my mother to be taken care of like this, to feel seen and heard, knowing that others care about her.

"I feel bad," my mother said. "I don't want them feeling like they *have* to do this stuff for me."

I told her they probably wouldn't offer unless they really wanted to. "It makes people feel good to give," I said. "So, you're helping them, too."

Having been raised to distrust others, I have had to learn how to become a better receiver of generosity myself. How to say yes to help, how to ask for what I need, how to trust that others want to help more than they want to harm. Kindness flows in all directions when we say yes to the goodness offered to us, feeling the rush of warmth that comes with any compassionate gesture. And we grow kinder toward ourselves, too, graciously letting go of our need to do it all alone, to be the helper, the one who gives. By saying yes again and again to small kindnesses, we reinforce the willingness in others to give, and the willingness in ourselves to embrace what they offer. It can feel vulnerable to admit that we need help, to let someone else into our lives. We might believe it should only be a family member or paid professional who looks after us, seeing love and kindness as reciprocal. But we have to remember that it brings us joy when we're good to other people. Compassion is not a purely selfless act. It is, in fact, one of the most powerful forms of self-love, the ability to give and receive, not blocking the abundance that wants to flow toward us.

Unseen Strings

Today, as I was walking home, I noticed a man up ahead with a pug on a leash. He seemed to be staring hard at me, and when we passed each other, his face brightened. "Well, look at this!" he said, waving. I smiled back, but because I didn't recognize him, and felt sure that I had never seen him before in my life, I kept going. I assumed he was acknowledging someone behind me, but when I turned to look, no one was there. This happens to me a lot nowadays—strangers mistaking me for someone they know because I'm so willing to smile and wave. But it wasn't always this way.

I spent my early years afraid to look others in the eye. I was shy, overweight, and gay, and because I was introverted, I didn't really want to be seen, risking recognition and judgment from others. It was much easier to pretend that I barely existed and was passing through this world invisibly. But something shifted as I grew older and stepped more fully into who I am. I started to feel a greater sense of belonging as I saw just how flawed my strategy had been, how much of life I'd been missing out on because of fear. By keeping my eyes down and staying in the so-called "safety" of a frightened mind, lost in fantasies or daydreams, I was giving up the simple pleasures—the way sunlight flashes in poplar leaves or how a woman looks down with total love at her toddler strapped in a stroller. By pretending to be invisible, I kept myself from noticing the light inside others, that glint in the eyes and hint of tenderness in everyone that never fails to remind me how connected we all are.

Now I do my best to take in my surroundings, even when it feels vulnerable to do so, even when I feel raw and exposed on a given day. I feel the salt and gravel beneath my feet on the wintry trails, the ice of the pavement as I step out of my car, and I try to meet the eyes of those passing by, nodding and acknowledging them. When we pay real attention to someone else, we honor them as a person and fellow being, and we make visible the unseen strings between us that keep trying to draw us closer together.

Secondhand Kindness

I was reluctant to leave the warm car that freezing morning Brad and I had driven forty miles to one of the few cafés nearby still open during winter. We dashed inside through the near-zero cold, dodging icicles hanging from the awning of an old factory that housed the bakery. Once inside, I felt held in the warmth of the place, with its fogged-over windows and sugary scents.

We stood at the counter like two kids choosing their treats from all the pastries laid out in rows beneath the glass—Boston cremes, lemon cookies, cinnamon rolls—and the server taking our order, who had gotten to know us a little, was sharing her favorites. "The chocolate babka is to die for," she said.

As I looked across at her, I couldn't help but hear the welcome in her voice as she rang us up, all of us a little worn around the edges by the long winter, but doing our best to keep going. At the last minute, we ordered a few curry soups to go, and then stood off to the side with our bags of pastries and steaming coffees we sipped with relish.

The whole energy of the place shifted, however, when a young couple walked in, trailing a waft of winter with them. They were bundled up in puffy coats like us, so I didn't see at first the baby with a hood thrown up over her head, resting in the woman's arms. I watched as joy spread from person to person in the restaurant—from the other people now waiting to order, to all the workers coming from the back to coo and say hello to the couple they must have known. Something about seeing that smiling baby's face wiggling in its mother's arms touched me so deeply that I began to wipe at my eyes. We were all softening in the presence of what felt like a bundle of hope for the future, a reminder that life always persists and continues, no matter what else happens in the world. I looked over at Brad and saw that he was also smiling, caught up in the joy, melting into the kindness of that moment offered to us on an otherwise gray day at the height of the longest winter in memory.

The World Calls to Us

Driving on the state highway, on our way to coffee, I thought the thing I spotted in the maple must be a burl, one of those huge knots in the trunk of a tree, or maybe a bundle of leaves that served as the nest of a squirrel. "What was *that*?" I called out, now sure I'd seen something special. And because Brad is an avid birder, his binoculars always nearby, he turned around and pulled off onto the shoulder. It took only a moment before we both saw it— a juvenile bald eagle perched on a branch, waiting for his chance to swoop down and feed on some roadkill. He did not yet have the distinguishable white head we're used to seeing, but he was the largest bird I have ever encountered up close. I could hardly believe my eyes.

Brad had already grabbed his binoculars and was peering across the highway at him. Even with my naked eyes, I could see what I couldn't help but think of as his *face*, his sharp eyes and curved beak, and his large yellow talons gripping the branch on which he rested for now. *Wow,* I kept saying over and over, more than a little pleased that I was the first one to notice this creature with his dark, ruffled feathers. Brad almost always sees the birds before I do, and can name them right away.

The eagle seemed to grow uneasy and restless the longer we sat there staring at him, and so—not wanting to disturb his meal anymore—we turned around again, this time pulling up right next to the tree where he perched, taking one last, long look at the massive bird, then continuing on our way to the café. But I felt changed after that sudden encounter for several days after, amazed at the way nature can still draw me out of whatever distracted state my mind happens to be in, bringing me back to the moment at hand, the world we actually live in.

When I first moved to rural Vermont to be with Brad, I thought I was a nature lover, deeply connected to the environment, but I realized I still had so much to learn, from the names of wildflowers that shiver up through leaf litter each spring, to the names of trees and birds, and the habits of animals that surround our house. I find myself looking out of windows more than I ever have, hoping to catch a flock of wild turkeys crossing the farm field, or a red-tailed hawk hunkered high in a tree, hunting at the periphery of the yard. No matter where we are, whether in the woods or in the middle of a bustling city, the world is always calling to us, and all we have to do to accept the gift is stay open to what we see.

You Are Enough

Yesterday I went for a hike by myself at a place called Haystack Mountain, about an hour from where we live. It took a lot to get me there—coming down from a very full and crowded week, I didn't much feel like driving all that way, and I knew that on a Saturday many other hikers would be there as well. But I more or less pushed myself out the door with my to-go cup of coffee, loading my bag with snacks and setting off. I figured I deserved the "indulgence" of a few hours away from home in the woods on a sunny and warm day in early spring.

You park at the bottom of a hill next to someone's cattle farm and then climb up an old dirt access road to get to the mountain. Judging by all the other cars parked by the field, I knew I'd likely meet a lot of other people with the same idea, but I had decided that I didn't mind. When I checked in with myself, I realized I sort of *wanted* to see others, *wanted* to be in a place where people like me were outside, finding joy in the quiet. And when I finally started up the rocky path, I knew I'd made the right choice. There were no leaves on the trees yet, and the woods were almost eerily still. Now and then one tree would rub against another, making a kind of creaking sound, or I'd hear a jet roaring overhead, bearing down on the treetops for a few minutes before leaving an even deeper silence in its place. I looked down at one point and saw my first wildflower, a trout lily in bloom—the tiny yellow blossom bent forward as if bowing down to the earth. The sun shone on the flower springing up out of last year's old leaves, with its own spotted green leaves now reaching up for the light.

I kept going for as long as I could and met a couple on the trail just as it began to get steep. The woman had a carrier strapped to her back with their baby held firmly in place, bobbing back and forth as they came down the trail. When they passed by with smiles and a wish for a lovely hike, I almost couldn't believe my eyes—how on earth was she carrying that much weight up and now down the mountain when I could hardly manage my own without huffing and puffing? Eventually, I paused by a stream fed by snowmelt, rushing over mossy rocks, and took a breather. The sound of the water drew me away from the trail until I'd found a wide stone where I could just sit a while and listen. I thought about how seldom I do things like this on my own, without my husband or a friend. Why was I so afraid to be alone, to practice self-care? I'm not sure how long I sat there bathed in the song of the flowing water, but it seemed to lift me out of time, out of my thinking mind for a while. I felt immensely powerful, too—I had followed my intuition to this place, had said yes to the desire to be outside in the sun completely alone, taking care of myself.

As I sat on my stone, I sensed a deep weariness in my body that I needed to obey, and which was being healed the longer I paused there by the stream. I watched a few golden beech leaves drift down from their branches and float on the surface of that clear water in a little pool near my feet. Soon, I felt it was time to head back.

I had the woods to myself a little longer before I ran into a large group of younger people just starting out on their hike for the day. I stepped off the trail to let them pass, and as they eased by me, I noticed the sweatshirt one of them was wearing. It had a rainbow across the front and the words *You Are Enough*. I looked her in the eyes and said, "I like your shirt, by the way." She giggled and thanked me. What were the chances that the universe had sent me the exact message I needed to hear at that moment, the message that I'd finally *felt* was true when I decided to come here for no reason other than to nourish myself and enjoy the day?

KiNDNESS PRACTiCE
FRESH EYES

Taking the time to look into the eyes of strangers we meet, or even loved ones we know well, can bring us back to the moment at hand, and signal our nervous systems to relax: we have enough time and the safety we need to tend to the people around us. When I find myself speeding past the person in the checkout line, or the librarian bagging up my books for me, I know I need to slow down and ground myself in our connection again. When I finally look into the faces of strangers, it's like waking up from a trance. I see them as fellow humans once more, inviting myself to notice whatever I can in their eyes, which can tell us so much about a person.

I ask myself: Are their eyes red-rimmed and tired, or bright and mirthful? Are they dulled from a day of work, or dancing with joy at a task well-done? Putting forth that small amount of effort helps us feel more connected to all the people we might be tempted to ignore or treat with detachment as we pass through the day. Looking into their eyes, we see them freshly, and often end up looking at the rest of our lives with a new perspective too, picking up on things we'd never noticed before. When feeling especially rushed and out of touch, you might try a practice suggested by the American Buddhist nun Pema Chödrön. While sitting in traffic or on a plane, for instance, you look at another person and say, "Just like me, that person craves happiness and joy. Just like me, that person wants to feel seen and loved, and avoid all pain." This can allow us to expand our empathy beyond the tight circle of our immediate lives. The path of kindness is really about paying just a bit of extra attention to the people around us, whomever they may be, and making the smallest shifts in perception that allow us to more fully inhabit our world.

Invitation for Writing & Reflection

Describe a time when you allowed yourself to pause and really look into someone else's eyes as you spoke to them, considering their lives. What did it feel like to share the spark of that connection, and how did it affect the rest of your day?

PART TWO
THE LOVE THAT'S GIVEN

Light for the Time Being

I am still learning how to be joyful even when I know others are suffering. I call my mother, who has agoraphobia, COPD, and multiple sclerosis, to see how she's doing, and she tells me she's not well. I can hear the strain in her voice, the phlegm in her lungs, the oxygen machine whirring in the background. And I am a thousand miles away, happy to be building a new house with my husband, the first place we can each truly call our own. Just the other night, I walked through what will be my office and peered out of the empty spaces where each of the windows will eventually go. I sat amazed on a folding chair in the unwalled part that will be our kitchen as late light broke through the trees, a few shimmering rays kissing the floor near my feet.

How can we be happy with so much injustice, so much still to be done to make the world a better place? How can I rejoice in my good fortune and also feel for my mother, let her pain mix with the joy that belongs in me as well? As Mark Nepo writes in *The Book of Soul:* "When blessed to be well, we balance the world by being conduits of light for the time being, as long as we stay touchable." When all is well with us in our own lives, we don't need to wait for the other shoe to drop, or feel ashamed of our good fortune. We fully accept and embrace where we are now, yet allow ourselves at the same time to be touched by the plight of others. We don't have to cause ourselves suffering just to match where they are either. We can stay in our joy, becoming beacons for those who need us, and trust that we may also be teaching others how to rest in those bursts of happiness without attachment, without shame.

I was talking with my wise therapist recently about all the work Brad is doing to build our house—organizing the contractors, ordering the things that we need, making the thousands of tiny decisions—most of which I just don't have the skills or experience to help with. I felt guilty and didn't think I was doing enough to deserve this concrete token of Brad's affection and generosity. Sitting across from me in her purple chair, she looked me in the eyes and said: "It seems your only job here is to accept the love that's given." My eyes welled up as the shiver of that truth moved through my body. I knew she was right: I can receive the gift that's offered to me, and stay in the joy, or I can stress about my unworthiness and all I haven't done to "earn" it, causing us both more suffering. I also took what she said as a larger commentary on our purpose as human beings: We are here to receive love from each other and the universal love that we don't have to do a thing to deserve. In other words, we are each worthy of love and belonging simply by being alive, trying to be present to both the joy and sorrow as they come.

Moments of Safety

*All of us were imprinted one of two ways: either the world is dangerous
with moments of safety, or the world is safe with moments of danger.*
—Deepak Chopra

Sometimes, we have to make a conscious effort to welcome the bursts of joy
that can frighten us because they can't be controlled or predicted. I have
often seen the world as an unpredictable and threatening place, and so,
like someone shutting off the valve to a gush of necessary drinking water, I
turned off what scared me as well as what excited me. But my husband, Brad,
has become my teacher in the way he allows almost every instant of joy to
spring forth, letting everyone else share in it with him.

After a long day of work at the farm in ninety-degree heat yesterday, he
pulled into our driveway and began wildly honking his horn for me to come
out of the house, thrilled to be done with another day and ready to go for
a walk together. As we wandered the farm fields together, I watched him
crouch over rows of ripe-to-bursting strawberries that we were picking for
his mom and dad, filling our largest metal bowl. Every few minutes, he'd
bring one of the plump, deep-red, still sun-warmed berries to his mouth and
eat, unable to contain his pleasure as juice ran down his dusty hands. Later,
when we went swimming, he stood on a rock beside the river and leaped
right into the deep pool of water with a splash that soaked me, too, where I
stood in my trunks, afraid of that first rush of cold. "Get right in there!" he
called to me as he came up for air, slicking back the hair from his face and
urging me to share in his relief.

It's never been easy for me to give myself over to the depths of a life
that felt like it held just a few moments of safety sprinkled in between the
many dangers. Growing up, I never knew if or when my mother would have
another panic attack in the grocery store, or when my dad would lose his job,
and we'd have to move again, staying with relatives in the city. I also knew I
was different from the beginning and became afraid that others in our tiny

Missouri town would harm me for being gay. I moved through my days at
school as if danger always lurked around the next corner. Which is to say,
I never learned to trust enough to feel it all—the joy, sadness, excitement,
fear, and tenderness I thought would drown me if I surrendered too much
and gave up control. Whether seated on the bank of a river or standing on
the brush-cleared land where we are building our dream home, Brad always
invites me to take the risk of showing exactly what I feel, to dive right in and
trust that I can swim in these safer waters with him.

Chicken Parmesan

It felt silly and wasteful to drive an hour each way on my day off just to pick up some take-out dinners from our favorite restaurant, Sissy's Kitchen. Yet I felt compelled to make this trip to pay forward at least some of the help and good fortune that's come our way in the past few months. Because my father-in-law is an excellent, experienced carpenter, he has come out of retirement to help Brad and me as we build our first house on a shoestring budget. He's gathered workers from among the locals he knows and spends hour upon hour each day at our land, checking every detail as the skeleton of the house rises from the newly poured foundation. And when Brad and I stop by in the evening, he proudly shows us around, pointing out where the windows and doors will go, and how much has been accomplished that day as we do our best to get the exterior sealed by winter.

Because both of my in-laws have helped us so much during this process, buying us little things for the new house, like a birdbath or barbecue grill, I wanted to do something special to show my gratitude. Ever since I moved to Vermont, they've seemed a little mystified by me and my deep need for privacy and solitude, which they sometimes take as a rejection of their affections. Yet, just as I have had to learn to receive their love and help, having been used to a very anonymous and independent existence in the city, they have had to learn that sometimes love looks differently than you imagined it would. I suppose I also wanted to surprise them with my gesture of kindness, and so I drove the hour there and back, sitting in traffic and navigating roadwork to bring home the chicken parmesan dinners we'd feast on that evening.

Brad and I don't always make the time for family dinners, but I was glad we did that evening. His parents seemed ecstatic to see us, joking at every turn, and even after working all day on our house, his dad stood at the stove and made buttery garlic bread for all of us. As we ate our delicious dinners, I thought they were perhaps made tastier by the effort it took to get them. Brad's dad said he even told the guys at the house site how far I'd driven to get us all dinner. I realized then that he had been bragging a little to the other men, and though he'd never use these words, he was feeling loved by his sometimes odd, writerly son-in-law. I sat alone later that same night before bed, thinking about the profound effects of our acts of kindness. We might have the sudden urge to do something for someone, yet end up rejecting it because we tell ourselves it "doesn't make sense," or we think it won't matter enough. Kindness is not always linear or predictable, and we don't need to explain or justify some gesture we feel drawn to offer. We simply trust the impulse, knowing all the ripples it will create.

I had so much work left to do that day, but I couldn't have been happier that I set it aside and chose not to listen to that critical inner voice that told me I really should be staying at home, I should be more responsible. I think about how much joy, laughter, and love we would have missed out on if I had not followed my intuition to share a simple meal with my husband and the people who have become second parents to me.

The Fire Is Always There

I was walking the trail at the park on a chilly summer morning when I met an older gentleman, his white hair tied back in a ponytail. He stopped right away, holding back his golden retriever straining at the leash to greet me. "Good morning!" the man belted out with a wide smile I didn't expect. "Feels like winter today!" I agreed that it did, looking down at the wool gloves I was wearing, and then said I wasn't quite ready for that. "Me neither," he said as he waved and walked on, the tags on his dog's collar jingling as we parted ways.

The sparkle I'd noticed in his eyes—as if amused by the sudden cold instead of annoyed by it—seemed to pass on to me after that, and I found I could hold the turn in weather more lightly as well. In fact, it felt like just a few watts of his bright inner light had shone on me, so I could see my way forward through the day a little more easily. I then passed that same light onto the next walker I came upon, flashing him a wide smile, and he looked just as startled as I must have when that man lifted me out of my own thoughts with his exuberant greeting.

This seems the way of life, when we let kindness guide us—to pass on what we've been given to everyone we meet. Even if they're strangers, it is in our nature to acknowledge and welcome others, especially if our own inner fire happens to be burning brighter that day. I noticed the gift of that man's light swirling in the cup of honeyed green tea I made for myself when I got home, in the dry, thick pair of wool socks I slipped over my feet later. I saw his spark leaping from me to every other person I met or talked to that day, even from a distance, until it dawned on me that the fire had been my own from the beginning. I just needed reminding that it was still there.

Invincible Summer

In the midst of winter, I found there was, within me, an invincible summer. And that makes me happy. For it says that no matter how hard the world pushes against me, within me, there's something stronger—something better—pushing right back.

—Albert Camus

It was a cooler, summer-turning-to-autumn morning as Brad and I walked the dirt roads around our house. He made fun of me because I kept stopping to move the tiny, neon-orange newts who had come onto the road after last night's rain, lifting their writhing little bodies to the safety of the other side. When a car pulled up behind us, we moved to the grassy shoulder, only to find when it slowed that it was our friend Virginia driving. We paused to chat for a few minutes, checking in on each other's lives—her husband's COPD, and the work being done on our new house. "What a beautiful morning, right?" Virginia said, looking around at the sun-struck trees and tossing her straight blonde hair now dyed a light shade of aqua that week. "I'd be fine if winter never came again," she said, and we agreed that we felt the same.

The coming cold had been on everyone's minds, and thoughts of hunkering down yet again for winter left us all feeling a sense of dread. During the last weeks of summer, I always feel like one of those wide-leafed maples—still green for now, absorbing all the summer light I can, and storing that nourishing warmth deep inside myself, in a place no melancholy can touch later on. Of course, what I've been storing, too, is the light of moments like this, when I can feel our friend wishing us well, telling us to have a beautiful rest of the day, using that word, *beautiful,* once again. Her smile lifted us both up, even after she drove away with a wave, blowing us each a kiss. In the past, I might have just let the warmth of our brief exchange fade, feeling it wasn't important. But now I believe that like the plants, like the Queen Anne's lace and goldenrod by the side of that road, we too can hold on to those bright moments that feed us.

I decided right then, as we said goodbye, to hold on to this kind of light—this *kind* light—to name it, seek it out, and turn toward it as often as I can, trusting that my own invincible summer will live on in me, no matter what future difficulties may come.

Lovingkindness

The other day, I lay in the loft of my writing studio, listening to rain pound the metal roof as I read an old novel—*The Big Rock Candy Mountain* by Wallace Stegner. I admit my attention was wandering as I steeped in the peace of that natural silence, until I came to a part in the book where a character receives a telegram and whispers to his friend, "My brother is dead!" As soon as I read those words, I put down the book, rolled on my side, and began to sob, releasing waves of unfelt grief for the loss of my own brother, Ron. He is not dead, but my mother and I have not heard from him for many years now. He is still in occasional contact with other relatives by text and social media, so we know he's alive and seems to be well, but he refuses to talk to either of us and has never offered a reason why.

He stopped talking to us about five years ago, after I confronted him about using my mother's credit cards without her permission, running up debts she'd never be able to pay back out of the small Social Security checks she lives on each month. Of course, I now wish I'd left things between the two of them as my mother had asked me to do, though I'm not sure it would have made much difference in the long run. My brother and I have always been such different people. We've gotten along but have never had as much in common as I would have wished. I was always closest to our mother, and he was closer with our father, so when Dad died over twenty years ago now, Ron was devastated. He has said to us that he felt like he lost his best friend. I'm not sure he ever fully felt the grief of that loss either, as we were both so young when it happened and trained by our culture as men not to show or even feel such deep and unraveling emotion.

A memory comes back from the months just before my father passed away, when I was too frazzled to drive us all home yet again from the hospital. Ron climbed into the driver's seat, lit a cigarette—even though he'd hidden his smoking up to that point—and let it dangle from his lips as he took full control of the situation, squinting against the smoke as he led us out of the maze of a parking garage. I remember thinking at the time in the backseat that both of us have had to grow up a lot more quickly than we might have expected because of our parents' various illnesses.

I have never thought of the loss of my brother as something I needed to mourn, I suppose, because I kept expecting us all to be back in touch and together again soon. But on that rainy day when I gave myself the permission to feel it, when I saw those words—*my brother is dead*—it dawned on me that this is a kind of death my mother and I both have to endure, even if he is still around, even if we might someday see him again.

After the tears stopped coming, and helplessness descended on me again that day, I placed my hand over my heart and brought to mind my brother's face—his shy eyes with the thick lashes, the way he smiles without showing all of the teeth we could never afford to have fixed growing up. With each in-breath, I inhaled all the worry, fear, sadness, and anger I felt, and sent it back out on each exhale as light and forgiveness toward him. This practice at least gave me the sense that I was taking action somehow, that I was doing *something*, especially since I trust in the power of love to ripple out into the world in ways we can't fathom.

Buddhists often use the Pali word *metta* to describe this practice, and it's translated as lovingkindness. It feels so true, this idea that there is a kind of love we can offer to each other, even while far away, deeply infused with kindness and care. That we can send it out and receive it on the very air we breathe, simply by doing what we would normally do to stay alive—inhale, exhale—but with the intention of wishing someone well. I don't know if Ron felt what I sent him that afternoon, and I don't need to know. But I like to think that even a scrap of light slipped through, and for a moment, wherever he was, whatever he was doing, he knew without a doubt that he was loved.

Estranged

In the dream, I was coming back from a walk in the woods near my family's old house on Tenbrook Road in Missouri. I stepped down the hillside above the backyard and found the ground covered in gnarled roots I'd have to climb over to keep from falling. When I reached the back porch, my mother handed me the phone. "Your brother wants to talk to you," she said. Even in the dream, I was aware of the fact that this was a major event, since my brother has not spoken to me or my mother in years. When I said hello, he answered in his old voice, but calmer this time, more sure of himself and seemingly at peace. He said something to me that I could not imagine him ever saying in real life: "I'm so awed and inspired to talk to you like this." It was a thrill for me to hear his voice, to feel reconnected and welcomed by him. The dream must have ended soon after that, because I remember nothing else from our conversation.

As I woke afterward and stared up through the skylight at the few stars left scattered in the sky, I began to feel anxious and fearful. Talking to my brother, Ron, like that felt akin to some of the dreams I had of my father, in the years just after his death. It felt like a visitation. And, of course, though other family members say they have texted with Ron, it's hard to believe that he is alright when so much time has passed since we last saw his face, much less heard his voice. Because I fear addiction is involved, I've often wondered what I could do to help. Friends and family have all said: "Just love him, send him kindness and light." While sending him lovingkindness certainly helps, it doesn't always feel like enough. Still, I know I've done everything I can to reach him, to clear the air, and it is up to him now to make the next move. I keep thinking about that word, *estranged,* and how cruel a term it seems when applied to a loved one—meaning someone with whom you were once so close, who has now become a stranger.

Perhaps my dream was only a message to myself: You miss your brother, you wish him well, and you wish he felt like talking to you. For a long time, I pushed thoughts of him away and refused to deal with the very real grief over this ambiguous loss that may be uncertain and unresolved, but is no less painful. I've now made it a practice to bring his face to mind at least a few times a day, if not more, saying his name and sending him the very concrete wish that he stay safe and well, knowing that he is loved. I've come to believe that my friends are right—this is what I can do, and it is more honest and active than trying to ignore things or pretend that our estrangement does not cut deeply. How can it not, when I still remember the little boy who used to cry every time his picture was taken, who slept in the bunk bed below mine wrapped in the same Batman sheets we used to make into forts on long summer days. How can I not send him every bit of my love when I still remember the man whose tender blue eyes and thick lashes could soften any heart with just a few blinks. My brother will never be a stranger to me, no matter how many years we go without speaking, no matter what unknown hurt he nurses against me. Maybe my dream was a gift meant to remind me that, no matter the circumstances, our true roots will always keep calling us back.

"You're Going To Be OK"

I tossed and turned on the hard futon bed next to my husband, listening to the waves of the Atlantic crashing just outside our window, having to pinch myself to remember where I was. Our friend Christy had generously lent us her family's cabin on the Cranberry Islands to escape the stress of work and building our house. While it had proven difficult for both of us to leave behind our jobs and all the work yet to do on our new home, we gladly accepted these few days away and made the long, eight-hour drive north to Maine.

As we waited for the mailboat ferry to take us to the island—the only way to get here from the mainland—Brad and I stretched out on the town dock, just taking in the waves lapping the shores of Northeast Harbor, basking in the pleasure of watching other people going about their daily business, sailboats ready for launch jutting their sharp masts into the salty air. "I could sit and watch the water like this all day," I said to Brad. I had no idea yet—this was his surprise for me—that our borrowed cabin rested on a precipice of Sutton Island; that in just an hour we'd be standing arm in arm on the deck, tracing waves as they curled in and out, and listening to the gorgeous sound of water forcefully sucking back all the rocks it had just washed onto shore—like the pop and sizzle of sparklers.

Later that night, despite being exhausted from having woken at 3:30 a.m. to get an early start, from hauling our bags a mile to the cottage from where we'd been dropped off, and from unpacking all our food for the coming days, I lay awake with the familiar buzz of anxiety like a shot of espresso coursing through my body. I am a creature of habit who loves routine, so even a trip to a magical place like this can easily unsettle me. I seldom sleep well the first night in a hotel or Airbnb, or even when staying with friends. After a chaotic childhood and decades of moving around as an adult from place to place and job to job, my body has trouble forgetting that sense of alarm that comes from being in a brand-new place, no matter how comfortable it might seem. I turned over again, making the futon creak and wheeze, and worrying that Brad would wake up frustrated with me for not sleeping—though he is rarely frustrated or angry with me. I kept focusing on my dry throat, convinced I was getting a cold. And what if I *did* develop a cough or runny nose, or something worse? What then? How would I get to a hospital? My mind spun out in all directions.

For some reason, I remembered the graffiti I've seen on an overpass in a town near ours. Every time I drive beneath those letters scrawled large in white spray paint, I can't help but feel better: *You're Going To Be OK*. As I lay there looking up at the wooden beams in the ceiling, I began to say it to myself over and over, a promise to the irrationally anxious part of my brain: *You're Going To Be OK*. Soon, to my surprise, I felt my body relaxing, my swirling stomach calming at last, the fear that I would get sick dissolving little by little, and if not disappearing, at least lessening in power. I turned toward the moonlit window, toward the lulling sound of the ocean, and didn't worry about how silly I sounded to myself, how utterly desperate I was to fall asleep that I'd made a mantra out of some random piece of graffiti I've passed beneath a thousand times.

Here's what I've learned in life so far: we can use what we have, or we can waste countless hours, days, months, and even years resisting the reality right in front of us—of these jumpy, fearful minds, and circumstances beyond our control. I could have spent all night telling myself I *should* be able to rest, and that I'm somehow broken because I can't, because I don't appreciate the gift of this cottage and a much-needed vacation with my husband. But that would have only caused myself more suffering. That spray-painted phrase came to me for a reason, and for once, I wasn't afraid or ashamed of comforting myself.

Shining Through

As I sit on a bench perched at the edge of this island in Maine, I think: the ocean is kind to these black stones stacked here on the shore. Every few moments, when the tide is coming in, they meet the force of the water splashing against them, and for the trouble of staying put and meeting life head-on, they are buffed to a deep gleam as soon as the sun strokes them. They are cleared of all the debris that clung to them and invited to awaken again and again to life with every incoming rush of freezing water now engulfing them.

The same is true for us, of course, though I've only recently begun to accept this. Just a few days ago, while forced to lie still in bed as the waves of unfelt emotions finally surfaced and began to buffet me, I thought about how, if we allow ourselves to be authentic, we are each worn down to live in our own ways. Like those stones, our hardness and sharp edges are slowly removed until we welcome all that washes over us, pleasant and unpleasant, even when it seems to threaten who we think we are.

Perhaps in our growth, the eventual goal is to become like water itself, to erode so fully into our love for the world, every piece of us flows in and flows out, knowing no distinctions and simply going around obstacles instead of pushing against them. I lean back on our friend Christy's bench sipping my coffee, seeing I have a long way to go before I come even close to stone or water in my ability to meet life head-on and feel what I feel in the moment, letting whatever arises slip through the cracks in the protective armor so many of us put on after difficult childhoods, traumas, and violence.

Yet, this morning at the breakfast table with Brad, I saw a glimmer of hope. We'd been talking about my struggles with anxiety, and how the fear and uncertainty of even this short trip almost kept me from a getaway we both desperately needed. Because I'd never been to the cottage before and didn't know what to expect, and because we had to prepare so much—buying food, looking at maps, planning our drive—I felt it might not be worth the trouble or worry. But Brad said that when we walked up the trail to the cabin, hauling all our bags, and I saw the ocean crashing and stretching out blue before us, he could see my joy shining through at last. I couldn't hide how surprised and thrilled I was to be here.

"I'm not always able to see that, you know," he told me, aware of how often my anxiety intrudes. Yet, he pointed me toward a small victory in the face of habitual thoughts of fear: if I practice feeling what I feel, and hold onto my joy instead of short-circuiting it with worry, I can get better at letting my authentic self shine through, rising to the surface in an instant like the glint of a single abalone shell the water kindly leaves behind on the beach for us to find.

Treasure Hunting

I didn't want to spend the morning digging for sea glass on that rocky beach near the dock where we were first dropped off on the island. I longed to be back in our cabin, curled up near the wood stove with a good book and steaming cup of honeyed green tea. But I could see what joy it brought Brad to slow-walk the shore where the tide had just gone out, scanning for glints of green, white, and the ever-elusive blue of bottle shards worn to smoothness. Every time he found a new piece of sea glass, he gasped like a little kid and held it triumphantly up to the meager light of the overcast sky. So, I stayed and dug with him, finding handfuls of glass pebbles, made joyful by his joy in this playful act with not a soul around and no cell-phone reception, not a single responsibility or chore for the next few days. Seeing the boy beneath the man I love revealed over and over reminded me how accessible such innocent happiness can be, if we create the right conditions for it, making time for rest and play and disconnecting from the outer world for a while.

Though I craved the warmth of our cozy cabin, I had to admit it also felt like bliss to taste the salty wind blowing against us, to watch the buoys sway back and forth, tolling their bells, to feel the silence and solitude wrap around us like the arms of a mother we haven't seen in months. We'd both been so consumed with work and building our house, we'd forgotten what peace a little time away could bring. It's been so long since I've seen Brad this happy, I had also forgotten what it's like to experience the secondhand joy of someone close to you, how contagious the drive to play can be, whether searching for sea glass, or snapping photos of the hilly, moss-covered floor of the forest, or simply standing on the lip of a cliff and cheering on the roaring ocean as it tosses wave after wave on the rocks below.

Eventually, I made my way home alone, and left Brad still digging on the beach for several hours more. But I will never forget his childlike gasps as if he had uncovered treasure. Or the light that slowly seeped back into his eyes the longer we spent on that island, away from it all, giving ourselves permission to drink as much coffee as we wanted, to hike the trails in the chilly rain. Those moments will remain as glimmering and smooth for me as the bagful of beach glass he eventually brought back with him—pieces small enough to carry with me in my pocket wherever I go, to remind me that happiness is largely a choice we make for ourselves, and sometimes all it takes is a little digging.

Play Is the Way

Brad and I were hiking in the Barr Hill Natural Area in northern Vermont on protected land that rises above nearby Lake Caspian and allows for views of distant mountain peaks as far away as New Hampshire. I was feeling agitated about the long drive home later that day, the rushed energy of just wanting to get back on the road. But we'd agreed this was the best way to spend the last morning of our vacation, walking up the steep gravel access road past sleek black cows and into the mostly evergreen forest filled with red squirrels that chirped like birds at our approach. Everywhere around the well-worn trail raspberry bushes well past their prime still clung to a few sour berries, and thick carpets of moss seemed to soften the very air we breathed.

By the time we reached the grove of spruce and fir trees where we paused for some water, all the restless energy in me had settled like sediment in a glass of river water allowed to sit still. We looked up and began to read a laminated sign tacked to a tree by the Nature Conservancy that invited hikers to stop here and build their own "fairy houses," urging us to keep them small (fairies are tiny, after all) and never to harm any living materials in the process of construction. I glanced around, and it was impossible not to notice all the little dwellings that had been built against larger stones, at the foot of each tree, and even in between their branches. The grove felt quieter and calmer than the rest of the forest, a magical place for sure.

"We should take pictures of these houses," Brad said, reaching for his phone.

"No," I said, "we should build our own."

And that's what we did for the next half hour, though it felt so timeless there, it could have been an hour or two that we spent gathering twigs, stones, and pieces of bark speckled with lichen to build our fairy houses. We stayed fully absorbed in the task, even when a few other hikers passed by and chuckled.

"A local tradition," an older gentleman said to us.

We just smiled and nodded, for once not ashamed that we'd given in to our childlike desire to make and create, to let ourselves get lost in nature as we all once did so effortlessly. When we finished, Brad explained his elaborate fairy home to me, complete with a stone that acted as both patio and floor and that would heat up like the ground floor in our own new house. I couldn't help but notice that the slanted roof was made of sticks he'd snapped precisely so that they all lined up, the same size and shape. The two structures I made were much more haphazard, placed against the trunk of a spruce, though I was proud of the chunk of bark I'd used as a door, inserting a tiny acorn as a doorknob.

Soon, we had to keep moving. Yet, as we hiked back to the access road, I now saw the woods differently. I noticed the shape of every stone, the length of each twig, and looked at everything more closely, as if I were still scouting for materials to build another fairy house. I felt more *involved* with the world around me, and perhaps that was the unspoken intention of inviting hikers to make something with the materials they find on the forest floor. It works the same way in life: we find more of what we train ourselves to see. If we're looking for all the ways the world is a broken and dangerous place, we will find no shortage of evidence. Yet, as I've discovered, if you make it your goal to hold on to more moments of kindness and compassion each day, you will find them—or you can make them yourself. In the past few years, I have realized that kindness is not only a practice, but also a training of the mind and heart to find connection, gentleness, and love wherever we look. I've also been called to expand my notions of what kindness is, so that it includes, for instance, stopping on a whim in the middle of a hike to build a few fairy homes, even when you feel rushed or impatient.

As we left the nature preserve, I noticed a blackberry patch just off the path and picked a few plump berries to feast on before we left.

"I didn't see these when we first passed by," I said to Brad. He just flashed me one of his wise smiles, letting me know he had seen them just fine before, when I'd been too caught up in my own grumbling mind to really take them in. I ran back to the trail, berries in hand, feeling more myself now, more in touch with that childlike place in me that has always known play is the way to rest, recharge, and clear away the stress of too much serious living.

Tending Joy

One evening, as spring made its slow way to us, the April sun finally warming the soil enough for things to sprout, Brad and I went for a walk, discussing our long days. I shared the difficulties of looking after my mother from afar, and he spoke of a wearying day at the farm, shuttling between greenhouses to water all the new seedlings. When we got back home, I felt bone-tired, ready to go inside and throw together a few salads for dinner. But he wanted to walk around our new front yard, greeting everything he planted last year, just now beginning to break ground.

I stayed by his side for as long as I could, as we admired the blades of daffodils reaching upward, ferns starting to unfurl, the butterfly bushes that birds love to hide in near the feeder, finally budding at last. But when we got close to the house, I decided I'd had enough.

"Where are you going?" Brad asked, hurt edging his voice.

"I'm tired, honey," I said. I looked back at him kneeling in the earth beside the berm he'd shaped himself with his tractor, having moved loads of topsoil and spread endless bags of cedar mulch. Still, I turned away, needing some time to recharge, leaving him alone in the yard.

It wasn't until the next day that I finally understood just how much happiness he finds in making an oasis of our yard. We had worked all morning and afternoon raking, clearing leaves and fallen branches, clipping back the thorny vines that take over the woods, when he got a text that his plants had been delivered to the farm. He would have to drive there, borrowing a truck to haul them all home.

"I can go and help," I said, thrilled to be out in the fresh air and full sun beating down. Of course, I had no idea what I was in for.

Potted trees and shrubs of all kinds were lined up by the farmstand as usual, ready to be sold this weekend when everyone would be excited to be outside. I figured just a few of them were ours. Instead, Brad wandered the rows of plants with pink and white tags flapping in the wind, pulling out dozens of pots that I then loaded into the truck—an elderberry bush, red raspberries, white raspberries, a spice bush, hydrangeas, buttonbushes, and the list goes on.

"Do you think you ordered enough?" I asked with a smile as I hefted yet another heavy pot into the truck.

"This brings me so much joy," he said. And in that moment, with his quiet yet honest admission, it all finally dawned on me. These plants represented work and responsibility for me, but they meant nothing but joy to him.

Brad has worked as a farmer for almost twenty years, and I have always taken pleasure in watching his interactions with plants, treating them like the living, thinking things they surely are—whether bean sprouts, cucumber plants, or tomato vines. He has a deep connection with the natural world I have always envied. So, of course, he wants to greet every plant in our yard as it struggles up from its winter sleep in the soil he spent countless hours moving around, mulching, and fertilizing. Of course, he feels excited to pick up the many native plants he ordered from catalogs and will give a home to in our yard. I'm still learning what it takes to grow things, to tend to them in a deeper, more patient way. But, over the years, Brad has taught me more about growing my own joy than anything else, showing me the essential kindness of valuing and making room for what brings me light, no matter what anyone else might say or think. Who else is going to name and ask for what brings me the most joy?

Because I grew up poor and still have a strong habit of "making do," I know that if I were in his position, I would have ordered a lot fewer plants. I would have said to myself that just a couple would be enough for me. But as I stared at that truck bed full of leafed-out flowers and bushes that would soon spread their roots around our new house, I knew I had some growing to do myself.

I also couldn't resent a single moment spent loading the truck that night with all those potted plants. It became a joy for me, too, bouncing along in the farm truck as Brad avoided the muddy ruts, knowing that we were now tending this joy together, nurturing a happiness that would keep on growing, coming back again with each new spring.

KINDNESS PRACTICE

CONNECTIVE JOY

Mudita is a Buddhist Pali word, usually used to describe the sympathetic or vicarious joy we feel in the good fortune and happiness of another. This is one of the most difficult forms of kindness to practice, however, because our culture often sets us up to compete with each other, even with the people we care about the most. The success and happiness of others can also cause us to question our own lives and to touch in on that soft spot of insufficiency that flares up when we see evidence of someone's joy and feel a sudden resentment at what they may have achieved.

When we choose to share in the joy of another—and it is often a conscious choice—we mentally set aside our own concerns and insecurities. It might take practice to reach the place of pure joy for a good friend's new job or someone's marriage, especially when we wish we had the same. Yet it can become second nature for us if we stay aware of our initial reactions and intentionally link up with the happiness someone else is feeling. I prefer to think of mudita as "connective joy," because it draws us closer together and keeps us from drinking what I call "the poison of comparison," when we compare the highlights of someone else's life with our own seemingly mundane, everyday experience. Ultimately, another person's happiness is never about us, and when we allow the light to keep shining on them, when we decide, in fact, to add to the light, that brightness falls on us as well. Kindness flows more freely in and out of our lives when we allow ourselves to feel with others.

Pay close attention to your reactions at the good news of others. Whether you hear about someone's happiness in person or on social media, do your best to note those initial responses. Write about a time when you could feel "connective joy" for someone else's good fortune, without envy getting in the way.

Earth School

Earth is forgiveness school.

—Anne Lamott

We have let our grass grow waist-high, too tall for the push mower. Lately, when someone comes over, I find myself making excuses for what I am afraid they will see as my laziness, this failure to do something as simple as mowing the lawn. But the truth is, I love wading through those riotous blades, daisies and red clover in full bloom as dew darkens my pant legs. I love the way everything alive at the height of summer clamors for its day in the sun with such irrepressible growth and energy you feel the season might never end.

I think I could learn everything I need to know from this earth we call home. The milky white stones pushed up by last year's frost teach me how to let myself be seen, how to shine in sun or snow or rain. And the blue jay imitating the call of a red-tailed hawk to scare off the rest of the birds from the feeder reminds me that we are not the only conscious, creative beings that inhabit the planet.

Mostly, though, nature shows me how to forgive myself for following my own path, for choosing to expose my true self in order to grow. I do not believe that plants and animals would ever speak to themselves as harshly as we often do, doubting and fearing their own nature. As D. H. Lawrence wrote: "I never saw a wild thing sorry for itself." I doubt the groundhog who feasted on the leaves of our black-eyed Susans feels a moment of remorse, or that the tiny orange newts I find everywhere in the woods spend a single second of their short lives berating themselves for not taking a better route to the ponds that will become their homes.

I think too much. I let my head guide me when my heart is the only true compass I need. We can learn to be gentler with ourselves, and, thus, with others, locked in their own private struggles. We can forgive ourselves for not finding the life that matches our fantasies, for not landing the so-called perfect job or partner, for not raising the perfect child or pet, for not having the perfect body. We can forgive ourselves for being the naturally imperfect human animals we all are and embrace the messiness of life all the more, holding joy and sorrow at the same time.

A Listening Presence

We lost our dear friend Phil yesterday. Brad came home early from the farm and burst into tears as soon as he walked in the door. I rushed to hug him right away, and we held each other in the mudroom as he told me that Phil's husband, Bob, was driving him to the hospital when it happened, his bad heart having finally given out. I didn't know Phil as well as Brad did; both he and his husband supported Brad when he was discharged from the military for being gay, when he came back to this small village ashamed and struggling to come out fully and embrace who he was. They became like fathers to him, showing Brad the only positive example he had of two men who loved each other.

For the rest of the day, we were both softer with each other, having cups of coffee and tea, then taking a long walk together in the afternoon, talking about how quickly and easily time passes. "It's Bob I worry about the most," Brad said. Both of us were just then trying to imagine the awful reality of having to live without the presence of the person who loves you and knows you most in the world. I could hardly bear to think about it.

We remembered Phil's sense of humor, his passion for life, and felt grateful that he got to spend this final summer at home with Bob, watering his flower garden and doing what he loved. I couldn't feel glad for much else that day, but it did feel like a gift, the way Brad and I would just stop what we were doing, as when we laid down our knives on the cutting boards before dinner and just held each other in the kitchen for several minutes. Or when we laughed and cried at the same time, remembering how Phil would often talk with his mouth full, little bits of arugula stuck in his dentures. Or when we went to bed and cuddled for a while, how I pressed my mouth into Brad's thick blond curls, feeling the texture and physicality of him, having been reminded once again of the limits of our bodies, the laws of time.

I also thought about some of the things that had bothered me this past week—emailing with a nasty editor, fretting about how much weight I've gained the past few months, almost none of my old jeans fitting me anymore.

What a lovely set of "problems" to have, I told myself now, the worries seeming so insignificant and far away, like little flickers of candles in a distant window. Phil's passing also reminded me of the loss of my dad, this fresh grief peeling back the skin of the old pain to reveal a wound that may change with time, but has never fully healed. As I sat with Brad throughout the day and evening, I was reminded that the best thing we can do when someone we love is deeply grieving is just to be there, holding the space for whatever comes up for them. We are there to listen, not to fix. Yet, the same truth applies to ourselves as well. So often we try to do and mend and cover up to move on too fast from a pain we will never be able to outrun. The best we can do for ourselves is simply to feel and become our own listening presence, welcoming all that comes up in us. When in grief, we need self-love and gentleness the most; we need to give ourselves the same space we'd offer to a loved one who's struggling.

That was just what I did once Brad fell softly asleep beside me. I lay there remembering my father, feeling the sharpness of that loss once more as I stared up at the stars glittering through the skylight, wondering where he was, then recalling that he is always as close as my own breath.

Window Moments

For the past few months, my mother and I have barely communicated. We have talked every week, sometimes several times a week, yet our conversations have stayed very close to the surface. Before she learned how to do it herself, I ordered groceries online for her and my grandmother, glad that I could have them delivered directly to their apartment door by clicking a few buttons a thousand miles away here in Vermont. But I was also saddened that our phone calls had turned so businesslike, my mother reciting a list of her needs for the week, or describing the symptoms of her various ailments—COPD, MS, Crohn's disease, agoraphobia. We were not communicating in the deepest sense of the word, which is *communing,* a kind of coming together in a sacred exchange of words, experience, and love for one another.

This weekend, all that changed when I called her, and I can't say exactly why or how. Perhaps the loss of our friend Phil reminded me of the brevity of life, or the memories of my father that have bubbled up lately called me back to what is essential. As she picked up the phone, I heard the excitement in her voice when she realized it was me, and she said, "Well, hello, my little boo-boo." I was calling to tell her that I would be busy for the next week or so with work, and she might not hear from me for a while. I could tell she appreciated the heads-up. As we chatted more, I sensed a larger opening, this sudden doorway through which I stepped into more vulnerability with her. It dawned on me that I had barely spoken about the house that Brad and I are building, perhaps because I feel guilty that we'll soon have a place of our own, something that always eluded my parents, who lost the first home they bought and were never able to own one again. But I hadn't given my mother a chance to be happy for me; I hadn't really let her into my life. After that, I realized that I seldom asked her any questions about her own life, or what she remembers about my father. I know as a teacher how powerful it can be to approach someone with a wide-open curiosity, to ask questions that show I'm interested in their point of view.

I asked my mom if she remembered the Christmas my dad found a bundle of money in the grocery-store parking lot with no one around to claim it. "We had no idea how we were going to buy you kids any presents that year," she said. "But your dad was always finding money when we needed it the most. He was always looking." We both recalled the honey-baked ham we were able to have for Christmas dinner that year, the strands of twinkle lights we bought to string around the house. "I still miss him like crazy," she said, and I began to ask questions about when they first met, how old she was, why my dad started hanging around her and her family. At the end of our conversation, which did feel like a true communion, she said, "This was so nice! I'm glad you called." Then my mother was more honest with me than she'd ever been before, apologizing for not being as present during our previous phone calls, telling me that her own pain and fears were getting in the way. She admitted she was having trouble managing all her anxiety lately. "I just want you to know it's not you. It's me and my stuff," she said.

I teared up then, shocked by her heartfelt and caring confession. I saw that, beneath the surface, I did feel fearful that my mother blamed me for the fact that I hadn't visited in a while, and that I'd been so busy lately with the building of our house and all my teaching. I know I can't expect moments like this every time we talk, but what a gift to offer someone when we allow ourselves to be seen and heard more clearly, when we feel safe and close enough to ask the questions that throw open the windows between us.

The Gentle Question

The other morning, Brad and I were bringing our snow tires up from the cellar. As he lifted each one up to me, and I rolled them out to the yard to stack in the backseat of the car, I felt myself getting annoyed, wanting to rush through this chore, thinking about all the work I had to do that day, though Brad wanted to stretch before we left, then stop for coffee and run a few more errands on the way. As he brought the last tire out wrapped in its white plastic bag, he asked me gently, "Are you feeling anxious today?"

With a resigned sigh, I said, "Yes," having just identified the feeling myself a few minutes ago. He gave me a tender, empathetic look and then we held each other for a moment on the steps of the porch.

There was a time in my life, just a few years ago, when I would have gotten angry at Brad for calling me anxious, as if it were an insult for him to speak the truth. If I named the anxiety I was feeling with him, my reasoning back then went, he would see me as broken and flawed, and it would have meant that I was doing something wrong. It always seemed safer and easier to push it away, pretend the worry and fear did not exist, no matter how clear those emotions must have been to others. It's taken years of therapy and simply opening to the truth of my felt experiences, however, to see that I'm just a person with a lot of anxiety. It is not me, and does not define me, yet, it will be a passenger on almost any trip I take, any risk I take, any time I step out of my comfort zone.

What Brad's question reinforced for me that day—and over the course of the next few days, as I anticipated a stressful trip back home to be with my mother—is the power of naming what I'm feeling, the permission of asking myself that same gentle question. As soon as the feeling was spoken out loud, it began to lose its hold over my actions, and I could pause and take a much-needed breath as we went about our errands. My mind still fixated on the future—What if our new house isn't built in time? What if the classes I teach at the college are cut?—but I was able to see each intrusive thought as just a manifestation of my larger worry for the well-being of myself and my loved ones. As we drove to the auto shop to have our tires swapped out, then chatted with friends at the café, I thought: What a potent act of self-love it is, to name what's coming up in us, and then to let it pass through like a cloud in the sky making room for some much-needed sun.

To Be Held

To be held by the light was what I wanted.

—Linda Hogan

Brad came downstairs last night as I was rinsing out our salad bowls after dinner. "Do you want a face massage?" he asked. I was a little taken aback. I'd been noticing all day how tension seemed to be gathering in my face lately, especially around the cheeks and temples, creating a slight twitch near my mouth. I'd been scrolling too much through online news, so fear and anxiety were present in every story I read, in every bit of air I breathed. I hadn't mentioned anything to Brad about the odd pain in my face, yet he often intuits when some part of my body is bothering me and will offer the necessary neck rub or shoulder massage that clears away whatever blockages have knotted up there.

I never like to ask him for a massage, especially now when he's working so hard at the farm to make sure that everything gets harvested and stored before the cold and snow start to hit. So when he offered exactly what I needed without my even having to ask, my eyes welled up with gratitude. I knew he was pushing aside his own aching muscles and fatigue at the end of a long day to tend to me. When I said something about how he didn't have to do this, Brad just shook his head and smiled.

I lay on the couch face-up, with my head cradled in his lap. He rubbed some almond oil into his hands and began to knead the skin of my face. We had never done this for each other before, and I sometimes have trouble surrendering to the deep intimacy of such moments, no matter how healing his touch feels. For about four and a half years before Brad and I met, I chose not to date anyone, with the intention of "working on myself," really embracing the loneliness and solitude of those long days and nights. But I think now that choice was also a way for me to avoid the intimacy that's always felt uncomfortable and a little threatening to me, because, to feel it fully, you have to give up the control that feels so familiar and comforting.

For a few minutes, my body stayed tense and clenched, until I slowly surrendered. As I relaxed into receiving this tender gift, remembering how lucky and blessed I am to have someone who cares about me so much, I also thought about how this letting go was good practice for everyday life, too. When a difficult feeling arises—despair, anger, grief—we can choose to place that emotion in "the cradle of lovingkindness," as Tibetan Buddhist meditation master Chögyam Trungpa once put it, allowing an unwelcome or distressing feeling to be held by something larger and unconditionally loving toward us. That idea had always seemed a little saccharine to me, yet, being held by my husband like that, I finally got it. Laying our anger or fear in the cradle of lovingkindness is just another way of saying that you can settle into a feeling, give into it, and let that part of you be loved, too, until it passes through.

The massage lasted for about twenty minutes, and once he finished, I opened my eyes, feeling like a brand-new person. "Your color is back," Brad said to me, wiping the oil from his hands. "You have this glow about you now."

I could feel it too, and it wasn't just from his touch either. In the midst of that complete surrender, I allowed myself to be held in a way I never had before, and this whole broken and beautiful world now seemed a kinder, gentler place to be in.

Heartened

My in-laws, who live just a few minutes away from us, close to the farm where Brad works, seldom ask me for anything. They know and respect how occupied I am with teaching and writing, and how much I need my privacy and solitude. Yet, I know I've often been rigid about protecting the boundaries of my aloneness, asking them not to show up unannounced, sometimes staying home when Brad has dinner with them. Which is why I was surprised when Brad's mom texted me last night to ask if I might help set up the next day for a tag sale they were having. I was both surprised and *heartened,* that wonderful, ever so slightly cheesy word, which suggests some deeper part of us has been touched and thus expanded, nourished perhaps by the attention of another. I told her yes, I'd be there as soon as she needed me.

After teaching online for most of that sunny September day, I was glad to get out of the house and use my body for something more tangible, helping Ann to haul tables out of the garage and carry furniture up from storage in the basement, laying it all out on the driveway and covering it in tarps. My mother-in-law has one of the kindest faces of anyone I've ever met, and she's always quick to smile in spite of years of hardship, raising her four kids and helping to look after her ailing parents. "I've gotta get a hug," she said when I showed up, pulling me close. I must admit, it has not always been easy for me to receive her openhearted love, in part because it hurts at times to be so far from my own mother. And because I'm naturally a reserved person, holding my feelings close to my chest, protecting myself more than I need to.

My father-in-law, Duane, came home while we were cleaning off one of his tables in the garage. "You're messing up my workshop," he said with a grin, and I told him I had nothing to do with it. We talked for a while about the new house, the placement of the windows, and I said how grateful I am for someone who can do all this intricate construction work, thinking of all those details that mystify me. Otherwise, I'd be completely overwhelmed by this complex, exhausting process. Duane's deep-blue eyes shone with pride then, and I could tell my words heartened him as well, told him that his often guarded, solitary son-in-law might be standoffish sometimes, but still appreciates his hard work on the place Brad and I will soon be able, for the first time in our lives, to call our own.

When I headed home, I felt so full after my time with these loving people I am learning to call Mom and Dad. I'm beginning to see that two things are true at once: I do need boundaries and solitude, and I also crave connection with my family, even if that means setting aside my own priorities and busyness to help them out, give back to these people who have given so much to us. Who bring us extra orange juice and organic butter when it's on sale, who keep our grass mowed and our driveway plowed in the winter, who drop everything they're doing when we ask them for help.

Human Quilts

Yesterday, I had the pleasure of sharing poetry with two different groups online. The first was a regular workshop I lead of fiercely supportive women who each week encourage one another in their creative endeavors, empathizing, listening, hands reaching up to touch their hearts when they feel moved by something one of us has written or said. It was our last session, and, as one of the members, Jill, pointed out, it has been such a comfort and source of hope for us to gather at this difficult time, for her to look out and see this human quilt of faces on the screen, there to fill ourselves up with creative energy and to feel the connection we are able to absorb, even from a distance. Another attendee, Denise, had spoken up only occasionally when the mood struck her; she'd usually just sit and listen. This week, however, she read a short but powerful poem about the way all of our voices linger in her mind for hours after, and said that she feels driven to sit in silence for a while once our meetings are over, simply to download all the shared wisdom.

Later in the day, I visited a college class on Zoom for a course called Introduction to Trauma Studies, taught by my friend Amy. It felt so enlivening to be among twenty-five younger people committed to working with others who have endured unimaginable difficulty and loss in their lives. I shared a poem of mine that focuses on self-care, describing it as a foreign language my life is inviting me to learn, if slowly, so that I don't always listen to that relentless urge in me to do more and more. I then asked the students to write their own poems and share their moments of self-care with the group. One young woman spoke of playing with her kitten in her college dorm room, while another described how running each morning keeps her in touch with her body's needs. Someone else spoke of the kindness she gave to herself by deciding not to caretake a friend struggling with addiction, refusing to wash his dirty laundry, instead focusing on her own. Still another brave young woman talked of her brother's early death, how that loss taught her to care for herself and seek out the social support she needed in order to thrive.

I couldn't see the faces of everyone who shared in the class, yet their essays and poems made another kind of human quilt, indestructible for the way their stories will always stay with me. Though I had felt anxious at first that I might not have much to offer this group of wise college students, I saw that I was wrong. I gave them each the listening presence of someone who genuinely wanted to hear about their lives. And because of that space I made, the class quickly became about what they were offering me and each other.

Both of these groups filled me with hope for the rest of the evening, in spite of the heaviness and grief embedded in so many of their stories. When we can come together in strong and vulnerable ways, we create the kind of trusting community that will keep healing the torn fabric of our world. When we see the authenticity of another or hear about how loss has touched their life, we feel less alone when we return to the inevitable griefs and disappointments of our own lives. That was certainly true for me when I stepped away from the screen last night and went outside for a walk. It had been a gray and overcast autumn day, but looking up above the farm fields at all the red and gold trees, I saw that just enough light broke through cloud cover to create a rainbow arcing above me. A sudden lightness over-took me then, and I began laughing out loud, full of faith for our future.

How Are You?

My friend Shari and I used to meet for weekly conversations in coffee shops all across Lincoln, Nebraska. We both taught at the same university at the time, so we often talked about work, but most of our conversations tended toward the deeper things of life—spiritual practice, compassion, and kindness in the face of fear or worry. One week, Shari invited a friend of hers who wanted to join in the talks. As we sat down at the table in the noisy café, I looked at the woman I had only just met and asked: "How are you doing?" She burst into tears and had to dab her eyes repeatedly before revealing to us that she hadn't been asked that question in such a genuine way in a very long time.

Mostly, we say, "How are you?" as a formality, a kind of social "hello," but when I ask it of friends, family, and even strangers, I always mean it. I do my best to leave space for a real answer, if someone wants to engage authentically and vulnerably with me. I've noticed lately that when I ask some people how they're doing, there is a moment of hesitation and a pause that seems to be asking back: Do you *really* want to know the answer to that? As long as I'm not caught in my own anxieties and have been tending to my own needs, I do want to know.

It occurs to me, though, that maybe a way of caring for each other might be to ask, "How are you?" with the *intention* of actually receiving a specific response. The other kindness we might offer ourselves and one another is to answer honestly, to share the successes and struggles we might feel too afraid to reveal. Not everyone will be present enough to give or receive such truth, of course, yet perhaps a moment of exchange like this can become a compass for us, leading us toward those authentic souls who *can* offer their support and be open about what they're dealing with right now, too.

Shari and I now live in different states, but still make time for phone calls and emails to share the books and podcasts that keep us sane and engaged. The other day when we spoke, I asked: "How are you doing?" And she said, "You know, I was going to say *just fine*. But then I remembered I'm talking to you. So, the truth is, I'm having a hard time with everything right now." Her simple yet honest response opened one of those window-moments between us, allowing me to ask why things felt hard and inviting her to share with me a part of her heart in which sorrow and joy, excitement and fear, always coexist at the very same time. As we spoke, it felt like we were swapping this same gift back and forth, just being there to hear the truth, knowing that the other person was willing to hold it with us.

Arms

The other night at a bookstore event, I ran into my friend Shari, whom I hadn't seen in more than two years. I asked if I could give her a hug and watched as something in her face, and in her whole body, seemed to relax, as if my question had acknowledged what we both secretly needed. As we leaned in and held each other close, I noticed that she was wearing her late grandfather's slightly oversized, bright-red cardigan, which I knew she usually kept in the closet to remember him. I pressed my face into the fiber, breathing in, more grateful than I would have ever guessed to be touched, and to touch back.

It should be no surprise, as I learned recently, that when we're forming in the womb, the first signs of our arms are these tiny buds that grow directly from the heart. This is why we feel pain in our arms before a heart attack, why we have this strange ache to wrap our arms around each other and press ourselves heart to heart, especially if we've been apart for a long while. It's almost elemental, this need, and though I would never have described myself as a "hugger" in the past, lately I find I'm willing to be the one who asks permission, closing that distance between us, and seeing the importance of this simple gift of acknowledgment we can offer each other.

As my friend and I parted ways that night, saying goodbye with brand-new books tucked under our arms, I felt a warmth spreading in my chest. There was just something about seeing a good friend out in the world again, catching a glimpse of her in her grandfather's red sweater that I know means so much to her. I felt what I can only describe as a sudden freshness, as hopeful as a tulip easing open on the first sun-filled morning of spring.

Circle of Warmth

Brad and I had dinner with dear friends last night, staying far past our usual bedtime because none of us wanted to let each other go. We sat around their large table, telling and listening to stories, laughing at their little French bulldog, Lila, who would sometimes yelp for no reason other than to get our attention, and who kept snapping at Albert's leather shoes because she thought his feet were about to attack the stuffed chipmunk she thinks of as her baby. Brad used to live above Gaetane's garage in a small apartment and got to know her, her daughter Alexandra, and her grandson Albert over the years. Talk drifted, as it often does when we all meet like this, to the time that Brad saved Gaetane's life. In English lightly accented by her native French, Gaetane told the story again of how she'd been eating cherries and dropped the bowl as she suddenly fell. Even from the distance of his apartment, Brad heard the bowl clatter against the floor and sensed that this was not a normal sound. He found her lying there, unable to get up or even move, and soon sought help from others, calling an ambulance.

As I sat in our circle of warmth drawn close around the table, I thought about how moments like these bond us to each other forever. When someone ignores the usual boundaries of privacy and stays in touch with their intuition enough to know when something is wrong, when help might be needed. When we care enough about someone to stay attuned, listening for a moment when they desperately need us. When we show up for one another in such an unconditional way, our life becomes tied to theirs, and the invisible cords that link us all as humans are suddenly visible, tangible, real. That evening, Gaetane said, once again, to Brad, "You are like a grandson to me."

Tragedies and accidents like the one they described can also show us that we are just one human family, "relative strangers," in the best sense of that phrase; we are all strangers who are related. It felt that way as we sat together around the table, and I sensed myself being drawn into their circle now, too, basking in the attention of friends I have missed so much over the past few years, our faces fully revealed to each other, my cheeks almost sore from all the laughter we shared long into the night.

Reach

This is how you get unstuck. You reach.

—Cheryl Strayed

Sweat seemed to stream from every pore in my body the longer I sat in the sauna built near our friend Christy's pond. Brad kept pouring cups of water on stones in the stove so that waves of heat and steam engulfed us. When I couldn't take it anymore, I stepped out in the chilly night and leaped with a splash into the icy pond below. I went under completely and will never forget the shock of cold in that fraction of a moment that felt like an eternity. Flailing in the heavy black water, I could not make my limbs move at first, and felt myself sinking until I willed my legs to kick again, bringing myself back to the surface. Then I forced my arms upward, as if through cement, reaching through freezing water to grip the worn wood of the dock and lift myself out.

Later, Brad said he wondered if he'd have to come in after me—I had stayed under that long—but I think I needed that shock to bring me back to life. As we sat on the dock afterward with our bare skin steaming, these words came to me: to live the life you want, you must keep reaching and reaching with your whole being.

We forget sometimes, submerged in the darkness of doubt, depression, or grief, believing there's no way out, that self-compassion can be a leap of naked faith, letting go of all comfort and safety, and just trusting that we will still be able to lift ourselves up again. I had done that years ago by going on a blind date with Brad, then falling in love with him, then deciding to move to rural Vermont without a job or a single connection, and without a guarantee that our relationship would lead to marriage. Yet, I sensed I had to try, I had to reach, I had to believe that the kindness of the universe would hold me and guide me toward the right path.

I've always disliked taking risks or embracing change that demands surrender and acceptance, yet reaching means breaking old habits in half, stepping out of the familiar patterns we are afraid to leave behind. Reaching is dating again after years of untouched solitude, applying for the job of your dreams, asking a loved one for help, or moving to a new place where you simply sense you have always belonged. It may take some time, but, after the leap, we can always find solid ground again, and we often emerge transformed and beaming, pleased with ourselves for at least making the attempt, even if the result is not what we expected or desired—and it almost never is. I felt that pleasure as I sat there on the dock, arm in arm with my husband, my blood pumping harder than it had in years, as if to warm the whole winter night around us and melt the ice-chips of every glinting star in the sky above.

Feeling the Trust

And sometimes you sense how faithfully your life is delivered, even though you can't read the address.

—Thomas R. Smith

We were nearly done with our sauna when Christy asked me to lie down on the wooden bench so she could pour cold water over my head. The fire blazed in the stove, waves of almost unbearable heat filling the tiny room. As Christy let the water fall on my forehead, she said, "I'm not really feeling the trust." I smiled, realizing that she was right: my eyelids had been twitching and fluttering as if I were convinced my friend would somehow harm me in my vulnerable state, that water would get into my eyes.

The revelation came like a blade of light. Trust has never been the basic way that I approached the world. I have not trusted that others will look after my needs, that I can take care of myself, or that life itself will take care of me. I saw that my faith in the kindness of the world had been like a Fabergé egg—easily shattered—and I didn't believe that simple hope could repair the scattered shards. Many days, it seems as if I'm waiting for some version of that sting of water in my eyes, that I am *expecting* to be hurt, insulted, or taken advantage of. This keeps me from releasing fully into the open arms of each present moment, unable to trust that it will catch and hold me because I am so preoccupied by what might hurt me, what might be taken away.

It is plain that we all face loss or pain in some form, at some point—but such awareness can morph into the useless armor of obsession that limits our lives and keeps us from true connection with each other and ourselves. I am slowly learning to take off the heavy metal of my own anxieties and allow myself to be more porous, to settle into a true relationship with each moment or person I encounter, as if I had invited it all—because, in a way, we *do* invite so much of what happens to us by the choices we make. I can't help but recall how pleasant it was that night in the sauna, when I finally let my sweaty body sink into the smooth wooden slats beneath me as my friend blessed me with cold pond water and the sure knowledge that deep trust in the kindness of our lives is the most practical tool we can carry with us.

Falling Together

Brad and I hiked through the cool morning, climbing the rocks of old river-beds to reach the cascading water of Lye Brook Falls. Though I'd been there before, I gasped again when I saw the beauty of that white water falling over layer after layer of shale, finally pooling at the bottom with a music that soothed my weary body. We sat on stone seats sipping hot coffee from the thermos we'd brought, mostly silent in our awe of watching that waterfall.

I thought about all the ways I've been worn by life in my forty years here, how the water of time has softened the sharp and rigid edges of my perfectionism, my need to please, my worries about what others will think of me. We are here, it occurred to me then, to show the world our layers and to let life flow over them, no matter how frightening, thrilling, or powerful it can be to surrender ourselves so completely.

Of course, love and intimacy complete this work for us most efficiently, but only when we give ourselves over to the process without holding back, without damming up the force and vitality of the elemental that moves through us when we truly love. I looked up at Brad, resting against his stone, cup of coffee tipped up to his lips as he stared at the top of the waterfall where it all began. How frightened I've been to let my own life tumble forward with this man's life, though I knew I had no choice from the first moment we met, the first day we spent together hiking a mountain, then having lunch, then having dinner and coffee because we couldn't stand the idea of parting ways just yet. Even then, I could feel the flow of my life beginning its unimpeded rush over all the layers that had led me to him. Though I have wanted to intervene and stop that flow at times—fearful, uncertain, faltering in my trust—still, the words that came to me the day we first met remain a part of the music that keeps me going.

I'll never forget walking with him on the cold streets of Northampton, Massachusetts, that December evening, where we were winding up our marathon first date. As he slipped his arm around my back, I heard a voice saying to me: *a love larger than the self.* Ever since, I've been a student of that love, which has sought to widen my path and show me that we are all molecules moving together, pieces of a love so large we can hardly imagine it. Love makes sense the most when we find ourselves humbled and right-sized by the majesty of the natural world, by a waterfall whose naked beauty reminds us that vulnerable exposure—being truly seen and heard—is the way we practice the vastness of this love within each of us.

A Love Larger Than the Self

It's been almost a decade since Brad and I met for the first time, sharing a whole day together that changed both of our lives. We first connected through a dating app, but because we lived in separate states at the time—he in Vermont and I in Rhode Island—it took us a month and a half to finally meet. In the meantime, we wrote long emails to each other, exchanging some of the deepest and most vulnerable parts of our stories. In fact, in his second note to me, Brad confessed that he had been discharged from the military when he was twenty for being gay, telling me how much shame this brought him when he was first sent home. Even though we'd never met in person, and were simply passing messages back and forth, I felt him opening up to me from the very beginning as if he somehow knew we were destined to be together.

We met on a chilly but sunny December day in Brattleboro, Vermont, about halfway between where each of us lived. I sat at a table in the bagel shop, pretending to be busy with my iPad while I waited for this mysterious man to show up—wondering if he would even come. Then I turned toward the bank of windows near the front door and glimpsed him through the glass. I saw him opening the door before he noticed me and felt a single word—*yes*—ripple through my entire body. We went on to have breakfast together, walked to an arts and crafts show, and hiked to the top of nearby Putney Mountain, where he told me birders gather each year to watch the hawks' migration. We sat together shivering at the top of that mountain on one of the exposed stones, staring out at the surrounding valleys. I had slipped off my gloves, and Brad took my hand in his, gently kissing the cold skin. I could have melted right then, and soon after we began to kiss for real, practically making out in broad daylight. When we stopped, nearly ready to move on to someplace else for an early dinner, a woman appeared seemingly out of nowhere.

"Would you two like me to take your picture?" she asked.

We both laughed, and Brad handed over his phone. It was as if she had sensed somehow that we would later want a record of this momentous day.

We each drove separately to Northampton—a bit closer to my home in Providence—and had dinner at a Middle Eastern place. I remember at one point while we were eating, I had this sensation of almost seeing into our future. I felt Brad again opening up to me about his family, and I thought: So, this is how it will always be from now on. I had waited for years to find a companion, someone who knew and loved himself, and had overcome the shame that afflicts so many of us to embrace who he really was. Even after dinner, however, we still were not ready to let each other go. We walked to a nearby coffee shop for the lattes that would keep us awake on our respective drives back home. And as we strolled along the cold streets of that college town holding hands, those words floated into my mind as if to explain the new feeling washing over me: *a love larger than the self*. We had only just met, yet I felt I finally understood what other people meant when they talked about unconditional love—the love that my parents felt for me, the love that I felt for them. I had always considered myself a seeker walking the sometimes difficult, zigzagging trails of the spiritual path, and I sensed the largest and most necessary teaching now coming my way at last: how to live from that place of love, which is always larger than the individual self.

Brad and I huddled together around a crowded table sipping our drinks in the café while students tapped at laptops and phones. I wasn't quite ready to go home with him—we had only just met in person, after all—but I kept hoping he would invite me back with him just one more time, because I suddenly knew I wanted to say yes. Instead, we spent most of our final minutes together staring with amazement into each other's eyes as if we couldn't quite believe our luck. At one point, Brad held both of my hands and shook his head. "You're gentle," he said, as if surprised. Like he finally had a name for what he'd been feeling since we first met.

It felt like the longest walk in the world when we headed back to our cars parked on a side street far from the center of town. Midway there, we stopped in the middle of the sidewalk and started to make out one last time. I knew people were passing by us because I could hear their voices and the rustle of their coats, but I didn't open my eyes even once. I couldn't. I was lost in those kisses, giving in to this man as I never had to another, and trusting that this larger love would carry both of us far into our new life together. Trusting that this larger love—though it's still difficult at times—was the path I had always been seeking. As I shivered in my car, marveling at the day we'd just shared and turning up the heat, I watched Brad leap out of his Corolla and come to my window. As I rolled it down, he said, "One last kiss for the road," and brought his lips close to mine.

We're Husbands

I confessed to Brad that I was feeling off last night, drained on a soul-level from giving so much lately as a teacher, worrying about my mom, and getting ready to release a new book of poems about gratitude and hope. I was thrilled about my new project, of course, but it's such a vulnerable, public act to put any kind of creativity out into the world. I didn't want to sound ungrateful or place my worries on Brad's shoulders, but I couldn't keep it all in any longer.

After clearing our bowls from dinner, I came into the living room where he sat by the crackling woodstove.

"Would you turn off the lights?" he asked. I flipped the switch, and we sat in the room lit only by the leaping orange and blue flames of the fire he had built, held in a cocoon of warmth together.

I told Brad I was still concerned about my mom being sick and unable to care for herself, much less my grandmother, who depends so much on her. I was worried about having enough energy to finish out the semester, and about getting sick myself because I knew I'd been neglecting my self-care. I told him how often, when I'm spiritually drained, I try to find meaning by pleasing others, digging deep to give more and more when there's really nothing left. Brad just listened to all of this, stretched out on the carpet, asking me questions now and then to clarify or pointing out how I might view things differently.

At one point in our talk, he reached out and touched my chest. "What does *this* tell you that you need?" he asked, pressing gently against my heart. That one gesture reinforced how much I've been in my head lately, not checking in enough with my intuition.

I told him what came to me as soon as he said that: "I need to shut down for a few days, stop trying to do so much for everyone else," I said.

"There's your answer."

I felt lighter the longer we sprawled there, firelight flickering across our faces. Though I was afraid I would sound neurotic, I also confessed that even in that moment, I was worried about burdening him with my problems, turning him into my therapist. He just looked over at me with a kind smile, his face filled with peace.

"You don't need to worry about that," he said. "We're husbands. This is what we do for one another."

That word, *husbands,* nearly made me burst into tears, as it seemed to hold all of my good fortune and gratitude for having found Brad, for our willingness to do the work of intimacy together, for the space he makes to hold all of my anxieties and fears, and for the fact that I've finally learned I can trust him with what I'm feeling, to believe that he won't run away. I thought about the old meaning of the word *husband*—to till or cultivate, to help things grow. Isn't that what we all hope for in a partner, someone who will help cultivate our best self, who brings us back to who we are at our core? I kept rolling what he had said around in my head for the rest of the night, feeling so much less alone, sensing the permission he was giving me to be myself.

KiNDNESS PRACTiCE
ACCEPT THE GIFT

Many of us might feel more comfortable being the one who steps into help, rather than the one who receives it. We often see the act of accepting help as a form of weakness, suggesting that we can't manage on our own. Yet, if we recall how fulfilling it feels to give to someone else, to lift them up when they need it or perform some small act of kindness, we might then have an easier time letting others tend to us as well. When we say yes to such an offer, after all, we make room for the feelings of connection that flood in when someone reaches across the space between us with a bit of goodness and care we might not have been aware we needed.

Sometimes, we have no choice but to receive. In such instances, life teaches us the practice of humility and the surrender necessary to meet the moment with open arms. A few years ago, I had to accept the lovingkindness of my mother-in-law, Ann, who stopped everything she was doing that day to drive me to the ER after a nasty tick bite left me fevered and barely able to move from bed. No one else was available, and I knew I needed her help. Not only did she sit with me at the hospital for hours, but she also took me to the pharmacy so I could pick up the much-needed medication that would soon bring relief from the tick-borne disease doctors discovered I had. After she dropped me back at home, I sat on the stairs leading up to our bedroom and just collapsed into tears of gratitude for what she'd done. I had always prided myself on being fiercely independent, and on being the helper and caretaker, especially given that both of my own parents grew sick at a young age, unable to care for me. The day that Ann showed me such unconditional love forever changed our relationship and helped to make me more aware of my own stubbornness when it comes to accepting the gifts others find pleasure and meaning in giving. I have since learned that it is a kindness, too, to receive something we want or need with grace, not pushing it away, remembering that we all benefit when we live from a love that's larger than the self.

Invitation for Writing & Reflection

Can you remember a time when you had no choice but to accept an offer of help from someone else? What was the situation, and how did it feel simply to surrender to their kindness?

PART THREE
MINDFULNESS IS KINDNESS

The Midas Touch

I'll never forget the time after a book signing, when a few friends and I
stood around the food and drinks table, talking at the reception. It was
late summer, and a plate of strawberries—my favorite—sat piled in the
very center of the table. I reached out and took one, slowly brought it to
my mouth. My friend Erin, who notices everything, called a halt to the
conversation, startling all of us.

"I'm sorry," she said. "The way you touched that strawberry." She
shook her head. "It was so tender! I just had to say something."

I was glad she made me see that, though I'd been on automatic pilot,
just satisfying a craving. Yet, somehow, there remained a part of me that
remembered the delicacy of each berry, recalling that they're so fragile in
the fields when ripe, they must still be picked by human hands. No machine
can replicate the carefulness of our touch. As I now know, from having
watched Brad on the farm, it takes an incredible amount of time and labor
to plant strawberries, spreading hay to keep the plants tucked away and
warm in winter, raking the hay in spring to keep them from molding, and
then nurturing them until they produce the sweet, red, summer-swollen
berries I used to buy only in plastic cartons from the supermarket without
a second thought.

When we pay kind attention to the people and objects in our lives,
we develop a sort of Midas touch. Everything we encounter then becomes
more precious and valuable, even the seemingly ordinary: the chipped and
stained ceramic mug from which I drink coffee each morning, the spider
plant whose sun-struck spiny leaves can't help but invite a gentle rubbing.
Or the strawberry I might have eaten that day without as much awareness, had Erin not said something. Though this kind of generous attention
goes by many names—savoring, mindfulness, reverence—one of the key
ingredients is the realization of the fleeting and fragile nature of everyone
and everything around us. Once we hold onto the truth of life's brevity,

kindness becomes the only sane and rational approach to everything and everyone around us.

Perhaps that's why, as our conversation resumed that day, I tasted the sweetness of that berry all the more, chewing it slowly, and reaching even more tenderly for the next one.

Take Good Care

On my walk back from the grocery store yesterday, I heard someone approaching from behind. "Excuse me, brother," he said as he passed by in his motorized wheelchair. I didn't think much more about the encounter until I reached the rehabilitation center around the corner. The man had paused at the bottom of the hill, and just as I was wondering if he needed help to get to the top, or if I should leave him be, he called out, "You think you could give me a push up this hill?" I told him of course I could. I got behind his chair and began to nudge him up the steep incline.

"It's not me," he said as we climbed. "It's this old chair. It just runs out of juice so fast." When we reached the ramp that led into the hospital, he told me he could handle it from there and thanked me. "Take good care," I said, tapping the torn vinyl seat of his wheelchair as he zoomed on.

But it occurred to me, walking home, that *I* should have thanked *him*. For the rest of the day, I felt grateful and pleased to have been of use to that stranger who no longer seemed like a stranger to me after the few intimate moments we spent together. How often are we given the chance to help someone in a way that taxes us so little and takes almost no time out of our day? What if we began to look for small ways like this to offer help without worrying about offending someone? So often I see people who might need a helping hand—a blind man standing at a busy intersection, or an older woman who's dropped her bag of groceries—yet, I hesitate, as many of us do, to get involved for fear of hurting their feelings.

Perhaps we need to make the leap to recognize that we are already deeply involved in each other's lives simply by virtue of being human and sharing this planet together. The offer of help, even if refused, can come as a blessing because it shows us someone was mindful enough of our well-being to stop and ask. And there will almost surely come a time when we will all need an extra push up whatever hill we can no longer climb on our own.

Light Seeking Light

A cold front had blown in the night before, so I was dreading the chilly bike ride to the farmers' market that morning. But by the time I arrived, the sun had begun to shine on all the tables with their stacks of sweet peppers, apples, and zucchinis, and I remembered why I came to the market each week. There was something about seeing and talking to the people who actually grew the fruits and vegetables I was going to eat, as I had learned from being married to a farmer. I loved knowing that the heirloom tomatoes I couldn't get enough of had not been trucked or flown in from elsewhere, that they were likely still hanging on the vine yesterday morning, gathering dew, soaking up their last few rays of sun.

I also came to buy from one of my favorite vendors even when she was selling things I didn't particularly need. She talked to me each week, asked how I cook things, mentioned my poetry, and she had the kindest green eyes I have ever seen, the light inside them seeming to seek out the light in the eyes of everyone who stopped at her stand. That morning, once I had bought my bunch of kale and bag of sweet potatoes, she turned to the man who had just rolled up in a wheelchair to her table. I noticed the hands resting in his lap, his fingers twisted and gnarled, barely usable.

"You need a jacket!" she called out as soon as she saw his short sleeves. "You want mine?" she asked, pointing to her fleece vest. He told her he was fine, but when she asked how he had been, I could see the relief wash over his face as he confessed that this was the first farmers' market he'd been able to attend in three years because of surgeries on his shoulders and legs. "Well, we've missed you down here," she said, smiling. Her kind eyes were focused on his as he tried to put the pepper he bought in his plastic bag. Of course, she came around the table and held the bag open for him, shrugging off his thanks as if all this were simply second nature to her, part of the job.

The Compromise

My task list was as long as my arm this morning, but I took the time anyway to be with Brad. He only gets a bit of time off here and there from the farm each summer, and almost always during the week when things are less busy. I'm used to setting aside several hours each morning to write and meditate, and I feel lucky to be able to start my days this way. But today I decided to give all that up, go for a miles-long walk with him, drop off some plants he bought for our new house, and then stop by his parents' place, where we shed our sweat-soaked clothes and went for a glorious swim in water that could not have been a more perfect temperature after the slightly cooler night. We swam quietly so as not to wake his mom, who was obviously sleeping through the balmy morning. While we dunked ourselves over and over, we hatched a plan to go out for breakfast at our favorite café.

I surrendered to everything, even when we sat outside the restaurant at one of the cast-iron tables, finishing up our egg sandwiches, and he said, "I'd like to drive to that nursery in Dorset to browse a little." I sighed inside, but told him that was fine by me, knowing that it would mean a beautiful drive through the deep-green and lush Mettawee Valley. When we got there, we walked through rows of blueberry bushes and cherry trees in search of the white-flowering viburnums he's been planting all around our house to attract bluebirds, cardinals, and cedar waxwings. They didn't have the variety he needed, so we ended up just wandering, easing through the steamed-up greenhouses where the scent of blooming roses wouldn't let me go until I bent down and inhaled from a few of them.

Back in the car, I was excited to head back home so I could get my phone calls out of the way and answer emails before an appointment that afternoon. "I think I might like to stop by the Equinox Nursery, too," Brad said, looking over at me sheepishly. This time I sighed out loud.

"I'd really rather go home," I said, feeling exhausted already by all that I had to do. "I'm sorry," I told him, and felt the energy in the car shift.

As we drove along in that loaded silence, Brad's brow furrowing in what I knew was frustration, I thought about how little time off he gets from the farm just to drive around, browse, and shop like this. I'm blessed with the much more flexible schedule of a writer and teacher who works remotely from home, so I often take for granted the fact of my freedom to do as I wish with whole chunks of my days.

I put my hand on his shoulder and said, "You know, we can go by the nursery if you really want to. I'll probably stay in the car, but you can take your time, just enjoy looking around."

His face brightened as I rubbed his neck and the back of his head. "That is a true compromise," he said, "and I really appreciate it. That makes my heart smile."

"Well," I told him, "I'm glad it takes so little."

It was true, I realized: as long as I wasn't expected to come along and browse with him, I would easily enjoy just sitting and people-watching for ten or fifteen minutes out of the day. If it brought him even a sliver of pleasure, then the time was more than worth it. I couldn't help but smile as I thought about what he'd said to me—*That makes my heart smile.* Have I really found a man who says things like that in total sincerity, a man who's in touch enough with how he feels to actually share something like that with me, without an ounce of embarrassment or shame?

As he parked at the next nursery, he rolled down the windows for me, and went off to look at all the potted trees and bushes wearing their little yellow Sale tags. I don't know if it was the spaciousness of the morning and the fact that I had given up all my routines just to embrace the moment, or if it was the energy of the whole world waking up in summer—but I felt so alive and present as I waited there for Brad, watching an older couple slowly climb out of their SUV, a clunky camera slung around the neck of the man. I saw him pause as soon as he walked into the nursery, snapping photos of an old Model T piled with hanging baskets filled with pink, purple, and white petunias. The whole scene was so vibrant and vivid, and I laughed to myself as I imagined the older man later posting his photos on social media, evidence of a moment neither of us would soon forget.

Nothing But Time

Because Brad and I often go to bed before the summer sun fully sets, we fall asleep to brushstrokes of light slanting across the sky and the fields around our house. Though the light feels endless at its height, there never seems to be enough time to do all we want in a given day—work the jobs we are grateful to have, pick strawberries, swim, cut each other's hair, talk on the phone to loved ones, walk the dirt roads whose dust climbs the ladder of sunlight breaking through the canopies of trees to greet us. I guess we all just have to make peace with doing and giving what we can in our limited time on this planet and let that be enough. We must trust that we are doing our best, and some days will simply feel as if they were built with a little less sand in the hourglass, always running out.

Last night, for instance, though I wanted nothing more than to sit in stillness, be quiet, and read a book as the cool breeze finally flowed down from the mountain, I saw that my ninety-year old grandma, Freddie, had called me, and knew that I had to call her back. I made the time, not out of fear or worry, as I sometimes do with my family, but from a deep desire to hear the voice of someone who's known and loved me my whole life.

Not long after my grandmother was married, she moved to St. Louis from rural Kentucky, having barely even seen a city before. Her husband, the grandfather I never knew, died unexpectedly a few years later, leaving her with five children to raise alone. She had only ever worked at picking cotton, and had never held a job or driven a car up to that point. Living in a still unfamiliar place, she was forced to work a string of factory jobs to raise her family and had to learn very quickly how to do all she needed to get by, from opening a bank account to writing out the checks for bills. All of this must be why she's thrived for so long. She only recently stopped driving and making her yearly trips back to Kentucky, but, luckily, she still gets around.

I sat outside on the porch steps as she told me about her five days in the hospital recently because she couldn't catch her breath one day after going to the bathroom. "They say I've got congestive heart failure," my grandmother told me. "Well, I already knew that! My old heart's gotta give out sometime, you know." She chuckled a little, then told me how, once she quickly recovered, she was washing herself in the hospital, eating whole meals again. "I even had a hamburger!" she said with all the excitement of someone describing a trip abroad.

I think this must be the source of resilience—to have made peace with your fears so thoroughly, to have faced them so completely that you can now delight in all the small things, sharing your stories and accepting the limits of your body and time. To see each day as *given* to you, and make use of it as best you can. Grandma Freddie has buried several loves, almost all of her siblings, and some of her children, including my father. Yet, talking with her out in the cool night where fireflies began to blink on and off, I felt her deep presence on the other end of the line. "I won't keep you any longer," she kept saying, but I didn't want to stop talking yet. "I've got nothing but time," I told her.

The Space of Waiting

I was on the most mundane of errands yesterday, sitting at the bank manager's desk and waiting while she finalized the paperwork and debit card for my new account. It was a few days before the Fourth of July weekend, so maybe that's why the bank buzzed with noise and activity and why it took the manager, Amber, a while to make her way back to me, stopping to help others along the way and explain why she could not meet with them just now. Her office faces a busier street in town, so I just sat there alone for ten or fifteen minutes, watching traffic flash by on that steamy day with gray clouds pressing down and threatening a thunderstorm that would hopefully break the heat.

It was then that I noticed a family walking by the bank together, the mother and her toddler daughter both wearing the same dress—a bright red top with a white skirt dotted with little cherries. The daughter kept twirling around, carefree, to face her mother and grandparents on the sidewalk, smiling and laughing, and I couldn't help but grin at the little girl and those matching cherry skirts.

As I sat there, I don't know why my eyes started to well up. I wasn't so much moved by the scene as I was grateful to take it all in without feeling rushed or impatient—the line of windows, the chill of the office from the A/C humming in the background raising goose pimples on my arms. It was a kindness to myself and everyone else in the busy bank to be content in the space of my waiting, not to feel I had better things to do, and just trusting that I would soon be taken care of. In a way, my time alone in the office was a break in the day. Had I not been forced to sit there, I would never have seen that mother and daughter in their summer dresses, and I wouldn't have felt the pleasure and deep emotion of witnessing the young girl's innocence and joy, the easy way she moved through her day. I would not have remembered that I, too, was once like her, as carefree and unselfconscious.

After a few more minutes, Amber breezed back in, explaining how to log into my online profile to view the account, and then checking on the status of the checks I'd ordered weeks ago. We were all business, but once we finished, I took a second to look into her eyes. "Thanks again, Amber," I said. "I know how hard you guys work here, and you always go the extra mile." Can you feel someone softening even from across the room? I felt it when she said to me, "Hey, do me a favor. You and Brad do something fun for the Fourth." She thanked me again for waiting so patiently without complaining.

Islands of Calm

Next time somebody says, "Sorry to have kept you waiting," you can reply, "That's all right, I wasn't waiting. I was just standing here enjoying myself."
—Eckhart Tolle

I was sitting in the car at a gas station that night while my friend Stella pumped our fuel. The station was like a small, lit island of calm in the sea of darkness around us, the sound of the freeway leading into town a distant roar. Next to us, a young man pulled up in a sleek black car with tinted windows, got out, and inserted the pump into his tank. He leaned against the side of his shining car, folded his arms and stared up at the moon and the few visible stars while he waited.

I was surprised when he didn't pull out his phone and scroll through messages to occupy those few free moments, or climb back into his car and crank up the music as others did. I thought of what Eckhart Tolle has said, that we are never truly waiting, and it is dangerous to label the experience as such because we can immediately grow impatient or bored. Instead, we can just say: I'm standing here or sitting here, appreciating this small break in the day. We can be present and grateful for the kindness of those rare minutes that are not filled with demands on our time and attention. Can we see waiting as a relief, a brief reprieve from the busyness of life? Can we welcome the chance to stand in line at a market, sit in a doctor's waiting room, or drive more slowly behind a car traveling annoyingly below the speed limit?

As I watched that young man just leaning there, closing his tired eyes and taking in the cool night air, breath by breath, I grew calmer myself. I get so used to rushing from place to place, thinking I need something to entertain me away from myself, when what I truly need is more of a pause between one experience and the next. When I'm hurried out of my natural speed, it can seem that my racing heart will never find a place of rest. Yet, in truth, there is always a tiny pause between each heartbeat, too brief for us to register. And in that small space of time, the heart is able to rest and restore itself. Life also gives us these gaps, and when we seize them, we serve as examples to others who might desperately need to slow down without realizing it. Making space for ourselves, we make small islands of peace in which we can all catch our breath for a moment before moving on.

Making Room

In the end, it is the reality of personal relationship that saves everything.
—Thomas Merton

There were plenty of other empty benches that summer afternoon, but the woman came and sat down on mine. I admit I was momentarily flustered by her sudden presence, my heart beating faster as I was drawn out of my solitary thoughts. Perhaps because I was now paying closer attention to myself, and to her, the rest of the world also came more alive for me. I noticed a bumblebee landing on each red flower of the clover growing near our feet, how the droning engine of his body began to buzz as he lifted off, then went quiet again when he landed. I watched a dragonfly hover in the air before us like a tiny spy plane, then dart off, as grasshoppers flung themselves from flowerbed to sidewalk to flowerbed. Even the poplars rustling around us seemed to be speaking some language I needed to learn.

The woman and I did not speak to each other. We were both attending a ten-day silent meditation retreat at the Insight Meditation Society in rural Massachusetts. On the land all around us, where I took long walks each day, I stepped over collapsing stone walls, which used to mark the borders of farms in the area. The truth was, after sitting still so much and without the pressures of being social with anyone else, I felt the walls in my own mind and heart beginning to crumble. We were there with almost a hundred other people, yet you never would have known it driving by or walking through the grounds. Silence had seeped into everything, and even at mealtimes, all you could hear was the clinking of silverware against plates and bowls.

As the woman and I sipped our after-lunch cups of tea, it seemed I could hear everything—her breathing, in and out, and my own; our bodies slowly digesting our food and rumbling now and then; her small sigh of gratitude every time she sipped the hot liquid and swallowed. Without speaking or needing to make the usual small talk, we could pay attention to each other and share a few moments together without adding anything to the experience. In fact, there seemed to be even more space since we knew we'd been discouraged to speak. In the past, I had often fantasized about living in a secluded cabin far away from the noise of life, believing that only emptiness and quiet could soothe my soul. Maybe it would for a time, but the longer I sat there on that bench, the more I felt I needed the communion and challenge of living close to other people to keep growing.

We can go off in the woods alone, or shut out the rest of the world, but our patterns, our unresolved and unfelt emotions, will always come with us. They will eventually work their way to the surface, with or without the company of others, like stones pushed up by frost in the fields around us. Human interaction is necessary for growth. We have to make space constantly for each other, and in doing so, we leave room for something much larger to enter us, too.

The Patience of Patients

Patience is wider than one once envisioned.

—Kay Ryan

Brad and I had just recovered from nasty summer colds. But about a week after our symptoms finally disappeared, he came out of the shower before dinner one night complaining of dizziness and vertigo. He'd been working all day out in the yard, planting our garden with the July sun beating down on him.

"You'll probably feel better after you sit down and eat," I said. I could tell, though, by the look on his face, that this was not what he wanted to hear.

"I don't want you to try and fix this for me, or calm me down," he said. "I'm telling you because I know my body, and something is definitely off."

I nodded and grabbed his hand. "I'm sorry," I said. "You're right. I'm not trying to dismiss or push aside what you're feeling. I'm just hoping it's not serious."

It's taken us a lot of practice to reach the point of honest and calmer communication like this. In the past, I'd have felt ashamed and reactive when Brad pointed out what he needed from me. I would have seen what he said as a criticism of me. I can admit that I've had a tendency over the years to try and downplay his sickness if it doesn't feel like an emergency because that was my role growing up with two parents who turned out to be ill much of the time. I was always having to bring them both back from the brink of panic about their health.

Now I'm grateful that we can share with each other most of the time what we feel and what we need, even if it's not what we're getting from the other person. In this instance, I saw right away that Brad was just asking me to be kinder and more open to what he was dealing with at the moment.

As it turned out, it was a good thing I listened. The next day, after breakfast and coffee, I watched him stumble back to bed, unable to move much or focus his eyes because of the dizziness and nausea that came with it. We kept hoping it would just go away, but I knew something was wrong. We decided to head to the Urgent Care at the hospital in town.

After a bumpy ride over gravel roads and streets still potholed from winter, I helped lead Brad inside so he wouldn't fall. I noticed the waiting room was nearly empty and thought: Great, this will take no time at all. How wrong I was, though, as we waited for an hour to be seen by someone, and Brad slumped down in his chair, needing to lie down. As we sat there, I watched a young man come in who said he worked at the Veterans' Home, holding a hand wrapped in bloody gauze pressed against his chest. As I overheard, he'd been changing trash bags when a sharp edge on a tuna can cut open his hand.

"It doesn't hurt much," he said. "I just need stitches."

He seemed so nonchalant and patient about the whole thing, sitting back and holding up his injured hand as he scrolled through his phone with the other.

I felt anything but calm, but finally, they called Brad's name, and led us to the back. After the bustle and rushed energy of everyone getting us into that tiny exam room, after the detachment of the intake nurse, and waiting again for another twenty minutes, the thoroughness and gentleness of the physician's assistant who saw him was a breath of life-giving air. Brad had been lying back on the table, and the young man named Spencer helped him sit upright with a gloved hand resting on the small of Brad's back. "I'm sorry," he said. "I'm not trying to torture you, I promise."

He checked all of Brad's reflexes and vision to rule out a stroke. "No facial drooping?" he asked us, and I shook my head no, thinking what a terrible question that was. He apologized again and again for anything that might make Brad more nauseated, especially the tiny flashlight he shone into each of his eyes. Eventually, Spencer said that what Brad had seemed peripheral; in other words, nothing serious to worry about. He prescribed some motion sickness medication and recommended going to the ER if things got worse, explaining that viruses sometimes affect the inner ear, and this must have been what happened.

"It's not unreasonable to go to the ER just to be safe," he said. "But I'm sure you two are tired of waiting."

Brad looked up from the exam table where he sat slumped again. He pulled on his ballcap. "I just want to go home and lie in my own bed," he said.

After a few more formalities, and questions to rule out other conditions, Spencer shook each of our hands and thanked Brad for being such a good patient. As we waited for yet another nurse to come with the final paperwork, and Brad lay back on the table with his eyes closed, I thought about what it means to be a good patient, the patience that's asked of each of us when we're not well, or when we're tending to a loved one who needs help. All we crave when we're in pain is a little kindness and someone's willingness to listen fully without judgment, without leaping to conclusions or offering immediate advice. Both Brad and his PA had taught me once more how to give patience to the patient, and how to practice presence at every turn with someone who's only seeking relief.

Today, Today

The more we commit to staying with the present moment, instead of spinning off into fantasy or distraction, the more we develop the tools for bringing ourselves back to kindness and connection. Many of us do our best to pause and take deep breaths when we feel ourselves spiraling out of control. I know some who wear rubber bands around their wrists and give them a little snap whenever their minds edge toward addiction or escape. One friend likes to look out of windows and watch the play of light in the trees or raindrops sliding down the slick bark. Because I have a very active imagination, I find that I also need to pay deep attention to my physical surroundings in order to keep from living constantly in daydreams. I feel the sensation of sitting in a chair or walking on the ground, how solid it seems beneath my feet. I look at the clock or the odometer in the car and see the number 57, which always brings me back to the present moment because it was the year my late father was born. I often think of what the Desert Fathers, an early sect of Christians, used to do whenever they felt their minds slipping into thoughts about a nonexistent future. They'd stop and say out loud, "Today. Today."

This came back to me recently as Brad and I sat on the wrought-iron chairs out in our garden. He was still experiencing lingering symptoms of dizziness and vertigo that were not going away. He'd been good about allowing himself to rest, though staying inside is never easy for an active person who's used to spending at least ten hours a day in farm fields or greenhouses.

"I don't seem to be getting better," he said. "And based on what I've read online, this condition could be chronic, could last for weeks, or months, or forever."

When we're unwell, it becomes easy to believe that our sickness will never go away. Even for those of us without a chronic condition, we start to think that nothing will ever change. Yet, I've come to see that change is the nature of everything, especially where our bodies are concerned, and I could tell that Brad had leaped into the future, ignoring where we were today.

"Honey, there's no reason to believe you won't get better. It just takes time, and it's only been a few days since this first started."

"I'm a realist," he said.

I told him I was, too, and it's realistic to believe that things will improve and change over time. I reached out across the metal table and held his hand in the dappled light, the trees around our house shifting overhead and the bumblebees busy at work on the nearby echinacea blossoms. The longer we sat there, the more I could actually feel him slipping back into the present, into today. I encouraged him to make it more of a practice to sit outside when he's feeling up to it.

"You're used to spending almost all of your time outdoors," I said. "This is healing for you."

Later in the day, I noticed him stepping out again to walk up and down the driveway, all the exercise he could manage for now. He also went out on the back porch and sat on the steps to check in with a friend by phone.

"You know," Brad said, coming inside, "it's almost like I feel better when I'm outside."

I smiled, seeing the light in his eyes as he decided to live for today, and let tomorrow take care of itself.

Relish and Release

It's true we must do certain things to look after our future—paying bills, packing lunches, prepping for a meeting or interview—but we don't need to conjure fictional scenes that may never exist, conversations that will never take place. So often our minds convince us that we are fortune tellers who can see exactly how things will turn out, and we waste precious hours of the day living inside our heads, dead to the vibrant world of possibilities always around us. When we start to believe we know exactly how things will turn out, we close off the many window-moments in life that allow us to be present to ourselves and each other.

Once we learn to surrender events to a future we can't predict or know, we find ourselves more open, attuned to creative approaches that only appear if there's room enough to receive them. I can't count how many times I have stood in front of a classroom and decided at the last minute to toss out a lesson plan I'd spent hours preparing because I sensed that the students needed a deeper, more genuine connection. Or because I remembered a poem or story that I sensed I needed to share with them. There is no safety net in such moments, but the reward of surrender is seeing the brightness in each face, excited to see what happens next.

When we let go of tomorrow, we gift ourselves with today. Then we have the space to appreciate the actual world. It's no accident that the words *relish* and *release* both come from the same French root word, *relaisser*, meaning "to let go of." What pleases us can also free us, if we have the heart space to bless its presence in our lives. Even if it's just the scent of a chicken roasting in the slow cooker, as it was for me this morning, when I stood at the counter and watched water bead on the hot glass lid. Or the tarp over the woodpile outside whipping in autumn wind, rippling and crackling, reminding me of all the fires we'll soon tend in the woodstove, gathered around its radiance and warmth. Our obligations might seem endless some days, but we can train ourselves to say enough is enough and relish doing something as simple as rinsing out a bowl, no longer lost in thoughts of what tomorrow will hold.

The Heart of Another

The heart of another is a dark forest, always, no matter how close it has been to one's own.

—Willa Cather

Brad and I were searching for a state park that day when we came upon the cemetery on the hill. All morning, the sun barely seeped through a hazy scrim of clouds, but the light shone fully on the wooden gate with chipped white paint that stood half-open as if waiting for us, inviting us inside. Each marker in the graveyard told of a love lost hundreds of years ago, but a palpable sense of peace had fallen over the land. As we crossed the mossy, sponge-like ground between stones, Brad confessed that he had come here once, years before, and sat alone on the same crumbling wall we were sitting on while a heavy rain fell upon him.

"What were you thinking about that day?" I asked.

"Existence," he said simply. I asked if he had come to any conclusions. "Just that it would be best to soldier on," he said, taking my hand and looking hard into my eyes. I knew what he was implying: this place was special to him because he had come here and decided to stay alive.

I'd known about his struggles with suicide in the past since the beginning, but his words took my breath away nevertheless. The idea that we might never have met, that he might never have touched all the lives he's touched with his farming and his gentle spirit, was almost too much for me to bear. I understood then that even the hearts of those closest to us can remain mysterious, uncharted territories. I might feel as though some piece of him has been with me since the day I was born, urging me toward him, but I will never know all of his joys and triumphs, fears and disappointments, just as he will never know all of mine. Like light slanting through clouds, our perceptions of the world filter through our individual consciousness and experience. Perhaps this is the kindest realization we can have in a relationship, that we will never fully know what anyone else has been through, and this is all the more reason to practice compassion in every moment we can.

We can lay aside our hesitations, gather what tools we can and venture into that dark forest of the heart, always without a map, and always on our own. We may cower at times, lose our way, call out for help, and stop to marvel again and again at the beauty no longer hidden from us. That gate stands partway open for each of us, and all we have to do is keep moving forward, keep choosing the path that takes us into the life of another, and thus more deeply into our own.

Bright Spots

I have learned to look for the bright spots in the darker, shorter days of winter. If I can find enough of them, and hold onto the light, I'm discovering that at the end of an evening, I can pause and say to myself, *this was a really good day*. This morning, for instance, Brad really wanted me to go for a walk with him, and even though I typically set aside the early hours for myself, he reminded me that it's a Sunday and nearly fifty degrees outside. Maybe, he implied, my agenda and task list could wait for a much colder day.

We parked at the town firehouse and began walking the loop we love to do on back roads near our new house, neither of us needing jackets. As we came up Maple Hill Road, we ran into Brad's uncle Mike and another family friend we allow to hunt on our property. We stopped and chatted with them for a few minutes, noticing there was no deer in the back of the truck, which I was secretly happy to see. Mike joked with Brad about the small backpack he was wearing with our water and jackets inside.

"What, are you afraid of getting lost?" he asked, and we all laughed, pointing out that you never know.

Not five minutes after we left them, we ran into Brad's dad driving the old Toyota Camry we had given him as a thank-you for helping out so much with building our house, for plowing our driveway and mowing our grass as often as he does. We stopped and chatted a bit more, and Brad joked that there's still a bit of time left in hunting season—just a few hours—for his dad to snag a deer. Duane shook his head, having tried all morning and come up with nothing.

We left him with a "Love you," then kept going, turning onto the road that leads to our new place, only to be stopped again by a stranger in a blue Saturn with a big fluffy Siberian Husky in the back. The older man had a wild white beard and mischievous smile as he asked if we knew that all the land around us belonged to just one person. We said we didn't.

"I think that's selfish," he said. "Not to share beautiful land like this with other people." He seemed to remember the two of us standing next to the open window of his car. "It's nice to see you guys out hiking, though."

We kept trying to be on our way, but the man seemed lonely and wanting to talk, so we let him tell us about how his family in Connecticut owns acres and acres of land nearby, and how his Husky is a "pain in the ass."

"Do you want a dog?" he asked, flashing that sly grin again.

"No!" we both said in unison and were able to break away soon after.

When we got home later, I could tell Brad wasn't feeling well, and was dealing with a sudden migraine. I had him sit on the floor in front of the couch, put on some Tibetan meditation music, and massaged his neck and temples, doing my best to bring some relief. He kept nodding off to sleep as he sat there, then lay down on the couch and napped for a half hour with the music of Tibetan singing bowls still going in the background.

I had started off the day thinking that I needed to be alone, and didn't want to be "disturbed" by anybody else. But after all this, as I lay in our reading nook, letting Brad sleep for as long as he could, I felt this was one of the best days I'd had in a while, all the firefly-flashes of connection adding up to something much brighter than I ever would have predicted.

KINDNESS PRACTICE
THE KINDNESS LIST

We are seldom encouraged to search out the many small and large kindnesses sent our way throughout the day. We often look instead for the ways we've been wronged or hurt and hold onto these events as a way of protecting ourselves against future harm. Yet, if we learn to stretch our definition of kindness beyond social niceties or politeness, we will find that each day contains its own string of kindnesses offered to us. We will also find there are countless ways that we might choose compassion and goodness for ourselves and others, too, especially if keep looking for those "window moments" as they show themselves, when we can reach out to another or do something gentle and sweet for ourselves.

Instead of seeing life as an endless list of tasks to rush through to get to the end of the day, we might look for those openings when we can give something, no matter how small it seems. We can also learn not to put off being kind to ourselves, believing it selfish to tend to our needs. Just today, I was luckily able to hold that intention in mind, taking the time for coffee, reading, and writing, then meditating after a long hot shower, and bringing cheese and crackers for myself to snack on while I waited for Brad in the car at the doctor's office, knowing I'd probably be hungry. I was able to pause and relish the slices of sharp Vermont cheddar on buttery crackers as I looked out at a wall of icy arborvitae and noticed a mother and daughter walking to the bus in the slanting sleet. I felt so full of gratitude that I took the time for that shower and all the other moments of self-care, which allowed me to be there for my husband and everyone else I encountered throughout the day.

Invitation for Writing & Reflection

If you're feeling especially down, or caught up in the rushed energy of a day, give yourself permission to sit down and make a few lists. The first might be a list of the ways you could be more kind to yourself when things feel overwhelming. How might you take care of yourself so that you're not wrung out and exhausted by the time you get home? You might then make a list of the ways that others have shown you kindness recently, no matter how slight, or how you have offered compassion to others in your life. The intention here is to allow ourselves to be held and surrounded by the kindnesses we might otherwise speed past, to remember that we are cared for, and that we, too, care about this life.

A Good Heart

Years ago, Brad and I sat across from each other at a scuffed table in Replika, one of our favorite cafés in Montreal. Mittens, hats, and scarves lay piled on a chair beside us, music blared from the speakers above, and the sounds of rapid-fire French spoken by other patrons threaded through the warm, espresso-scented air. We held hands across the table, looking into each other's eyes and smiling, comfortable with the silence between us. Only a few months before this, we had met online, exchanging the lengthy emails that would lead to our first meeting, and to this spur-of-the-moment trip across the border together—technically just our third date, though it already felt as if we'd been seeing each other for years.

As he sipped his milky flat white and I drained my Americano, we had what I like to call a heart-to-heart, for the first time confessing our surprise at having met each other, how hard we had fallen.

"I never expected this," Brad said, describing how much he'd been hurt in the past by other men, and especially by his most recent ex, who had cheated on him and lied throughout their time together about hooking up with other guys online. "I didn't think this was even possible," he said. Tears filled his eyes, and he shook his head, trying to blink them away. As soon as I saw him crying, my own eyes welled up, too.

I gripped his hand and moved closer so he would hear me over the noise. "I will always take care of your heart," I told him, not even knowing where those words had come from.

"I promise to do the same for you," he said.

We sat like that for a while, wiping our eyes, just being with each other in what felt like an eternal present moment. I looked around at boots leaking snowmelt and salt onto the tile floors, at the glass bar where the cook placed perfectly arranged grilled cheeses and steaming bowls of butternut squash soup. I knew there was nowhere else I wanted to be, and while I'd had instances during the previous weeks of wondering what I was doing with this organic farmer from Vermont, afraid of how fast we were moving, I felt a deep faith well up from inside me that all the decisions I'd made up to this point were absolutely right.

I remembered what my friend Shana back in Rhode Island had told me when I confessed that I'd connected with an organic farmer online and was about to meet him in person for the first time.

"We keep trading these long, detailed emails every day," I said. "It feels like the real thing."

She sat her cup of tea down on the table between us and looked up at me. I could see years of pain and frustration behind her eyes.

"Just be sure you find someone with a good heart," she said. She closed her eyes, shook her head—as if tossing away bad memories—and said nothing more.

Her advice felt sound, and I have certainly followed it. But I also believe that each of us already has a good heart, and that basic kindness is our nature. The goodness just gets covered over sometimes by busyness, bitterness, greed, and confusion about the truth that our lives are so intricately woven together as to be inseparable. Even with strangers, I have come to see that kindness is mostly revealed in sudden glimpses and glimmers, like a spot of paint rubbed away to show the pure gold waiting beneath. We can never predict when we'll catch sight of those glimmers, but if we stay on the lookout for them, if we keep believing that we mostly don't want to cause suffering for ourselves or anyone else, then we will see more than enough evidence of those good hearts beating in the chests of nearly everyone living their lives alongside us.

A little later, I stood in the café's bathroom at the sink, splashing cold water on my face and staring into the scratched surface of the mirror at that blurred version of myself. My eyes seemed to glitter as they looked back, and just in case I didn't get what was happening, I said out loud to myself, as if to a doubtful, fearful friend: "This is the real thing. *This* is what you've been waiting for."

It took me a few minutes to come out of the quiet bathroom back into the busy café. I needed to stand there and really *feel* what was happening, to know that this kind man with a good heart was, and still is, exactly the one I had longed for during all those lonesome nights. Here he was at last, sitting at a table in Montreal, and here we were, having committed never to hurt each other, when we can help it, about to step out again into the snowy morning, his mittened hand resting on the small of my back in a gesture of protection and love.

Compassion Is a Verb

I'm looking out at the hillside beyond my window and marveling at how it seems so much softer just past dawn. How the fuzzy, white seedheads of goldenrod seem to invite touch from this distance. Some might see a late autumn landscape as barren and depressing, but this morning at least, it seems honest to me, true to the cycles of what it is meant to do—let go, transform, and give up for a while the relentless searching and storing of light that happens each summer. I am thinking, too, of the ways that, when we are true to ourselves and honest about what we're feeling in a given moment, we become so much more compassionate toward ourselves and others. The Vietnamese Buddhist monk Thich Nhat Hanh once said, "Compassion is a verb," by which I believe he meant: it is an active, daily practice and something that we can generate at any time if we pay attention.

Self-compassion, which I've found is the first step in showing kindness to others, is perhaps one of the hardest practices to start and maintain. I remember once telling a friend that before I step into a classroom to teach, I like to pause outside the door and say a little prayer for all the students, asking that I be as present as possible for them. My wise friend looked at me for a moment, her head cocked to the side, and asked, "Do you ever pray for yourself?"

That gentle question really unsettled me, and I realized it was true that I did not often think to include myself in my own circle of compassion. The same thing happened last night. I usually like to meditate for twenty minutes or so before bed because it helps me sleep and lets the noise of the day die down a bit in my mind. Once I finish, I often sit with my hand pressed over my heart, bringing to mind each person in my life who might need some extra care that night. I just let the names and faces come to me organically and then offer love and light to them on each out-breath. Ten years ago, I would have laughed if you'd told me I'd be doing this practice each night, but I can't deny that, when feeling isolated from friends and family, it does make me feel better.

Last night, my friend's words came back to me—*Do you pray for your-self?*—and though it felt strange at first, I sent love to myself as well, hoping that my fears for the future might calm a little as I slept.

It can be a powerful and emotional practice to set a place for ourselves at the table of kindness and compassion, to see that we are as deserving and in need of care as all the others we include in our prayers. It's essential to remember that compassion is not just about serving others or rejecting any difficult emotions that come up because they seem unkind. As Sharon Salzberg writes: "We don't have to struggle to be someone we are not, hating ourselves for our confused feelings. Seeing clearly what is happening is the ground out of which compassion will arise." We don't have to worry about how we define ourselves, if we lose our mindfulness and presence for a while in the midst of an argument. As long as we see what's happening within us, even if we can't quite stop the momentum of anger, fear, or frustration, we can actively allow our compassion to become more loving toward the flawed and beautiful humans we meet, including ourselves.

Becoming the Parent

What I regret most in my life are failures of kindness.

—George Saunders

If we're doing our best to stay aware and present to our lives, we will likely recall our failures of kindness much more vividly than the tenderness we gave. This is one reason I make it a practice to capture those acts of grace and compassion I've followed through on, writing them down in a journal, so I can train my mind to find the goodness among my many missteps along the way. One of those failures came back to me again recently.

My mother had just moved into a new apartment with my grandmother back in Missouri, and I was visiting from Vermont, driving her to doctor's appointments and helping her tie up loose ends with the move. We had stopped by the Social Security office that afternoon so she could fill out the paperwork to change her address and phone number. After running around all day, I was feeling frustrated by how slowly my mother had to move with a tiny tank of oxygen slung over her shoulder like a purse, the way she had to pause every few steps to catch her breath, and needed my help just to get in and out of the car. We finally stood at the counter in the office where she held the change of address form.

"Can you do this for me?" my mother asked, her forehead beaded with sweat.

Wanting to empower her, I said no. I thought she could handle it. She is not that old and has only occasional slips of memory, so I try to help her stay as independent and active as possible. This has been a challenge since, when he was alive, my father took care of almost everything for her and all of us. Our whole family depended on him as the sole provider, the one who could once fix anything, who could go out and somehow make enough money for groceries that week, even when his paycheck from the plastics factory was not enough. I couldn't blame her for being used to that dynamic.

She began to fill out the Social Security form in a shaky scrawl. When I saw what she wrote, I said, "Mom!" in a whispered shout. "That's your old address." I felt my anger rising up—not at her, of course, but more at the fact that she couldn't do a simple task like this on her own anymore.

She sighed and tossed the ruined form into the trash. We took a new one out to the car so she could sit down and concentrate, but my annoyance also followed us. When she asked me to repeat her new phone number—which she had just recited from memory a few minutes ago—I threw up my hands, and shook my head. My mother began to cry softly in the passenger seat. I looked down at her hands, now trembling even more than before, and felt like the worst son in the world.

"I'm sorry, Mom," I said. "I just want you to be able to do things like this for yourself."

She wiped her eyes with a balled-up tissue pulled from her purse. "It's my brain," she said. "It's so foggy sometimes."

I knew this was a result of her multiple sclerosis, but I also remembered how often she has trouble doing things like this when she's fatigued, when she's simply ready to be back home. She finished filling out the form without a mistake, and I ran it back inside for her. In the end, though our moment in the car together still brings me a hint of shame, it also taught me that I have to be gentler with my mother as she gets older. It was one of those pivotal times when I realized we were entering a new phase of our relationship, and I was becoming her caretaker, even if I did live thousands of miles away. I resisted that truth at first, but soon saw that from now on, I'd have to become the parent, treating her as tenderly as I would a child who has to learn a whole new way of being in the world.

Mindfulness Is Kindness

It takes bravery to train in unconditional friendliness.

—Pema Chödrön

Kindness is one of the underpinnings of mindfulness, a daily practice that helps us pay deeper attention to the passing moments of our life. If the idea behind a mindful approach to living is not to judge our experience as good or bad, pleasant or unpleasant, then the point is to be kind to ourselves and others no matter the circumstances we find ourselves in. When we speak of kindness, we often think only of giving to those in need, or doing good deeds, but we forget that it's nearly impossible to serve the world if we cannot show that same regard and care for ourselves.

The first time I felt truly kind toward myself, perhaps since I was a child, was during a solo trip to Bogotá, Colombia. I had taken all my savings one summer after finishing graduate school and flew someplace that frightened me, taking on an adventure that I knew would demand my full presence. Though I still managed to distract myself at times, mostly with fantasies for the future and thoughts of past wrongs, I began to do some real soul-searching in my tiny hostel room. Day after day, I meditated and prayed and walked the city streets so much I wore through the soles of my sneakers. Slowly, I could feel the layers of resistance and fear growing thinner, if not entirely falling away. I began to feel reborn—raw and vulnerable, yes, but also open to the color and character of that country where I barely spoke a word of the language. I was open to every unfamiliar face I passed; open when a group of guys threatened me on the street; open when shop owners laughed in my face at my poor Spanish; open to not knowing my way through the maze of streets, or even how to insert my card to use the train. And though it felt painful at times to be so exposed, I knew this was how I wanted to live my life from now on; not running from things, but meeting them head-on with a smile and no judgments.

One day, I stumbled into a vegetarian café owned by an Argentinean woman. I could not believe the array of foods I could choose from, including glasses of freshly squeezed passion fruit juice for which I would return daily again and again. The owner was the first person to speak to me in English during that trip, and the first person with whom I'd exchanged more than a few words in several weeks. She must have sensed my need for connection, because she asked me where I was from, if I were a student, and why I'd come to Colombia—which was not necessarily easy to explain. "You will visit Argentina someday, too, yes?" she asked me, finally noticing that we were holding up the line at the register. I promised I would.

I laid down my tray of food and went to the bathroom to wash my hands. Standing at the sink, I looked up into the mirror, where I seemed to see my true self—the self behind my face—for the first time in many years. Even beneath the full beard I'd let grow in, I recognized my late father's face too, and the resemblance that family members had always been pointing out in the past was finally obvious to me. I stared into my own eyes with immense gentleness and said out loud, not caring if anyone else could hear me: "You and I are going to be good friends from now on, aren't we?" It was like speaking directly to my soul.

Though I'd never have said so at the time, those words were a promise, that I would do my best from now on not to be so hard on myself, always bent on achieving and being the smartest person in the room, and not to abuse my body anymore with cigarettes and drugs and too much drinking. I would try to do only those things that feed me deeply and help me stay connected to myself and the world. I have, of course, veered off the path now and then since that day, but the kindness I offered myself in that moment of openness has rippled out over the years and across every aspect of my life, allowing me to help others see themselves in the same unconditionally friendly and mindful way. If we can't begin by being friends with ourselves, how can we ever expect to do the same for others?

Needing Your Voice

Yesterday my mother was caught in what I call "emergency mode." She had called me several times, and when she couldn't get through, she called Brad, who was working in the farm fields and unable to answer. When I saw I had missed her many calls, I thought something must be wrong and phoned her back right away.

"What's going on?" I asked, a little breathless, with only about fifteen minutes before I needed to teach a class.

"I'm thinking of going to the hospital," my mother said almost nonchalantly, as if she were telling me, "I'm thinking of getting a new TV." But she had that anxious edge to her voice I've learned to recognize when she's especially worried about something.

Feeling rushed and a bit frustrated that my mother often seems to have these emergencies when I'm most busy and don't have the space to be there for her, I tried to sound as gentle as I could, suggesting that what she was feeling was fear. This sort of behavior is a long-standing pattern for my mother that's been present ever since I was a child, and, though it is humbling, I now recognize some of the same reactions in myself, like hyperfocusing on my health when I'm really stressed about something else. My mother's a very anxious person and tends to believe that every small thing wrong with her might lead to the worst-case scenario. Again, like me, she has an excellent imagination.

One Christmas a few years ago when I was visiting St. Louis, she felt a little weak and off-kilter, so she convinced me to take her to the ER. We spent Christmas Day not baking butter pecan cookies together and constructing a gingerbread house as I had planned, but instead watching home improvement shows in her tiny room, waiting for tests to come back and doctors to make their rounds. After about five hours at the hospital, which I spent either sitting by her bed or wandering the hallways and searching for the best vending machines, a doctor finally came in and said it looked like she had "a touch of flu," and prescribed antibiotics.

Needless to say, that day tested my patience, but I also understood that she was living alone at the time and was afraid because I was leaving again for the East Coast in just a few days. She'd be alone again, and what if something terrible was wrong with her?

I thought of that long-ago Christmas Day as we talked on the phone, and I told her with all the compassion I could muster: "Mom, I have to be honest. Unless something really serious is happening, you're better off at home."

"I know that," she said, her voice finally breaking, "but I feel like if I don't do something, I'm gonna die here. I can't even make your grandma's food. I'm too weak and can barely eat anything besides peanut butter toast."

I recommended that she sit down and write out everything that's been bothering her so she might describe it to her doctor. But I asked her to give it a day and see if she feels better then. I know it's hard for her, as someone who's not well, living with COPD and MS, and being on oxygen all the time, to help care for my grandmother, who's had several strokes and can't do as much for herself. Yet, it sounded to me like all she really needed was a break from the daily pressure of all that. It's hard to know that anyone you love is suffering, and even if I didn't think it was an emergency, I also didn't want to downplay her pain. I listened for as long as I could and told her several times how much I loved her and missed her.

"Thank you for calling me back," she said. "Maybe I just needed your voice."

Those last words she said before we hung up nearly cracked me open, and I probably would have sat on the couch and had a good cry if I hadn't had to teach a class. The hardest part of all this is that, at a less busy time, I'd have been gearing up to visit them, since I get more time off around Thanksgiving. And I'd have been able to give my mom some relief—taking over the cooking, laundry, and shopping for a few days at least, cleaning their apartment and doing some of the small chores with which they struggle. All I could offer in this instance, however, was my voice, which seemed to break through her frustration and fear, even for just a few minutes.

Seeking Center

I had just landed at LAX, one of the busiest airports in the world, to visit with friends. As I stood outside, waiting for my ride in the perpetual sunshine among palm trees and the honking, speeding cars, limousines, and buses, I watched all the travelers reuniting with loved ones. But one young man in particular caught my attention. He was surrounded by a pile of bags, and his unruly black hair and unshaven face both suggested he had just finished some long journey, perhaps having backpacked someplace far from here. His tattered jeans also seemed to hang off his thin frame, barely held up by the worn leather belt looped loosely around his waist.

Like the rest of us, he waited by the curb, searching the line of cars until a much older woman pulled up in an SUV and jumped out, long gray hair flowing behind her. She ran to the back to help him load his bags, and though she wore a tailored, spotless black pantsuit, she couldn't keep from hugging this young man I took to be her son. She kept bringing him close, then standing back a little to look in his bright blue eyes and rub his uncut hair. The bags loaded, they were about to hop into the car, but then the son called out to his mother, and she rushed toward him again. They held each other for what seemed like several full minutes until a cop blew his whistle to keep the traffic going, and they moved on.

I'd just left my own mother behind in St. Louis, never knowing if it was going to be the last time we'd see each other. Yet bearing witness to this exchange between mother and son, I was able to bring her with me into this new place. I was able to tap into the centripetal force of human love, so that I felt as if my mother and I were somehow sharing that moment together. Centripetal force (from the Latin *centrum,* meaning "center," and *petere,* meaning "to seek") is the force that keeps a body going at the same speed along a circular path, ensuring it stays aligned with the center. We travel in circles, through the sky, toward and away from each other, but love is the grounding energy we can seek in each of our moments that brings us back to center. We find it by looking inward, but also by looking outward, paying attention to its many expressions in the world around us. It pushes us forward, giving our lives purpose and direction, and no matter how fast or far we stray from each other, the centripetal force of love is always there to bring us back to the one true path.

Back on the Path

I lost it at the dentist's office that day. I had brought my mother to her appointment and sat flipping through magazines, waiting for her for hours. I was hungry and impatient by the time she emerged, and then the receptionist presented us with an itemized and very detailed list of expensive dental work that my mother would need to have done in the future. I should have kept quiet and not let the overwhelm get the better of me, but I began asking questions about which procedures were absolutely necessary and which ones we could skip, since my mother did not have dental insurance, and I would be the one paying. The receptionist, an older woman with carefully permed hair, fervently pointed out that *all* of the work was needed and started to explain why, but I simply cut her off and wouldn't let her finish.

"Look," I said. "My mother's on a fixed income. We can't afford this." Then I said that if the dentist could not accommodate us, we would go elsewhere.

By now, my heart was leaping out of my chest. As my mother and I climbed into the car and headed home, I instantly regretted treating the woman that way and could not believe how I'd forgotten to pause and breathe, taking a backseat to that initial rush of anger and frustration.

All through lunch, I couldn't stop talking with my mother about how I wished I'd acted differently, could not stop replaying the tense interaction over and over in my mind. So when I went out again to drive to the market, I knew I was really headed back to that dentist's office. I had to wait a long time to see the receptionist again, and as I sat in the same place in the waiting room, staring at the photo collages on the wall, I once again felt my heart beating so hard I was sure it must be visible even beneath my coat. I did not want to swallow my pride and apologize, did not want to sit there in such discomfort, rehearsing what I would say to this stranger. I wanted to stew in my righteous rage and justify my behavior so I could get on with the day's many errands. Yet I also knew that if I wanted to stand in my values, I had no other choice. "Come on around," the receptionist finally said, waving me to the side of the counter where we could talk.

"I just wanted to say I'm sorry for being so rude to you earlier," I told her.

"Well, I—thank you," she stammered out, a little taken aback. "But I didn't think you were rude. You were just concerned about your mother."

"That's true," I said. "But it's no excuse. I don't like treating people that way. I know you were just doing your job, and I appreciate it."

I placed my hand on the counter and said again how sorry I was.

"You're gonna make me cry," the woman said, tearing up, and laid her hand on top of mine.

Because I was receptive and more willing to listen now, she explained to me the different payment options, how procedures might be combined into one visit since my mother doesn't drive. I confessed that it was just me now looking after my mother, since my father had died years ago, and my brother was out of the picture, unable to help. Everything had changed, not only because I had opened a door between us, but also because we had literally touched each other, had bridged some gap. I was now looking into her eyes, paying attention to her puffy gray hair, how her small mouth shaped each word.

After I left, I felt free, as if my wheels had been realigned by listening to that insistent voice inside that told me I could not rest until things were made right with this stranger who became a stranger no more. She had written her name, Connie, on a card for me, and I'll never forget it.

I couldn't wait to tell my mother what had happened. But when I came home, she also had a surprise for me. Connie had called to say that they'd made a mistake in calculating the costs of my mother's procedures and would be taking another $1,500 off the original price. I had not expected this to happen when I went back to apologize, but I was not entirely shocked either. I have learned that things like this occur when we treat each other with the dignity and kindness we all deserve as interconnected human beings. When we let others see us as vulnerable people who sometimes stumble and lose our center, and when we humbly own up to our mistakes, we step back onto the path, able to receive the kindnesses that come our way.

The Greatest Prize

Kindness toward others and radical kindness to ourselves buy us a shot at a warm and generous heart, which is the greatest prize of all.
—Anne Lamott

I recently entered a period of my work life when free time became scarce, and my days grew busier and fuller than they had ever been before. Though I managed to set aside a few precious hours each morning for the daily writing and meditation practices that keep me alive and sane, I quickly adjusted to this schedule, this more public way of being in the world, in spite of my being an introvert who's more comfortable with solitude and silence. Those lamplit hours at my desk, watching the sun crest the mountains each morning, became a lifeline for me, where I could rest for a while, writing in my notebook, sipping coffee, unrushed by the noisy demands to come. And knowing that I had at least twenty to thirty minutes of sitting meditation, during which my only job was to watch and count my breaths, allowed me a sense of expansiveness and perspective I would have been lost without.

Soon, however, I noticed a blank week in the upcoming month just before I was set to travel again for work, giving readings and presentations all over the country. I had not consciously kept those squares open on the calendar; it just so happened that no requests for teaching and no deadlines fell on those days. At first, I thought I should fill up the week. What would I do with so much time on my hands, and wouldn't it be better if I scheduled some meetings I'd been putting off, did something more "productive?" Yet some wiser and kinder voice in me said, in its customary whisper: "Keep the time open. See what happens. You deserve some rest." I still didn't quite trust the voice, but because I'd been taking care of myself enough to be aware I was being offered real wisdom, I chose to listen.

The first weekend of this unexpected break I could barely get out of bed. I thought something must be wrong with me at first, but soon saw I was probably just exhausted. It didn't take long to know that was true, to feel the fatigue that took over. We grow so accustomed to matching the unsustainable pace of the outside world that we lose track of our own more natural speed, our own soul time. We forget to check in with ourselves, knowing we can only go so fast and do so much before the body begins to shut down, and our spirit feels like a snuffed-out candle, all its brightness gone.

Even though restlessness still swirled through me, I decided that every day I would fulfill the obligations I absolutely had to, but then would do no more. I'd invite my body and mind both to slow down and take long walks on the forest trail near our house where spring was beginning to green the grass and send wildflowers up through the softening soil. As I gave myself the essential kindness of just being tired, the guilt over "doing nothing" or "not being productive enough" began to fade, and the world seemed to greet me again, welcoming me into its arms. I noticed the wildlife also returning to our small corner of New England—ruby-crowned kinglets, hermit thrushes, and even a broad-winged hawk perched in a branch outside our house in the evening, hunting its nightly meal around the bird feeders we keep stocked with seed. One night before supper, before the light had fully left the sky, Brad and I spotted a porcupine sauntering through our front yard, feeding on the leaves of the pricker bushes whose thorns obviously didn't bother him. Looking out at that odd but adorable creature with his spiky brown and gray quills gave me more pleasure than I ever would have expected and rooted me here in my place for the first time in months. The more we pause, giving ourselves the space in our crowded lives, the more we're here to receive the world's countless gifts of attention.

It can be easy to fall into the habit of only giving to others and brushing aside our own needs. When we fall out of touch with ourselves, we don't just need a bit of tenderness to bring ourselves back; we need *radical kindness,* the type of deep self-care that can feel overly indulgent and even trans-gressive, but only because we're used to directing our energy outward, believing that is the way to become a better person. I couldn't be more grateful that I chose to turn inward during that time and listen to the still, small voice that's always there to guide us.

Open Hearts

A friend told me once that, after her beloved grandmother passed away, while everyone else squabbled over which valuables should go to whom, she decided to take two heart-shaped lockets—one gold, one silver—that were broken and that no one else wanted. I thought this a fitting symbol for her relationship with a brave immigrant grandmother who taught her how to love the world, especially since the clasp on each locket was so worn out that neither heart would close.

Her story reminded me of the day of my father's funeral. A terrible snowstorm the night before had backed up traffic for miles on the interstate as I drove to the funeral home. I desperately had to use the bathroom and tried to hold it, but had to pull off the highway at a fast-food place near the exit. I stood in the endless line to get the key to the restroom, feeling so isolated in my pain from everyone else ordering their coffee and egg sandwiches, going about the usual daily routines. But then I noticed that the young woman cashier wore a gold locket around her neck that had sprung open. The photo she had kept inside was apparently gone. In my grieving, emotionally drained state, wondering how I would go on living without my father, I thought the emptiness of that locket matched exactly the vacancy in my own heart. I had awakened that day with a visceral sense that some essential piece of my body was missing, that there was a hole in my chest that nothing would ever fill again.

Now, I see the locket as a message encouraging me to embrace all the facets of this one life we're given, all the pleasures and the griefs at the same time. Maybe, in that difficult moment, my father was saying: Don't ever shut your heart, no matter how much pain you feel, no matter what you lose. Maybe he was telling me not to crowd my life with keepsakes to remember him or keep him close—because he would always be with me. Even now, I can hear him saying: Keep your heart open, and the world will fill it.

Breaking Open

To be bruised or broken open by the loss of a loved one, an illness, or being forced to find a new job can seem like the worst kind of punishment. In the brokenness of extreme change and the uncertainty that follows it, we feel the pain of total exposure to life's elements. Yet what if this is the only way we can truly share our gifts with others? What if breaking open is the only way that the light that nourishes us can get in through the thick skins we often prefer to keep between us and the rest of the world?

There is a very old fig tree outside my dear friend Stella's house in Los Angeles. One summer, I happened to be staying there when the fruit dangling from its ancient limbs finally ripened. Each day, we'd wake and take coffee outside to see if any of the figs had gone soft enough overnight to pick. Most of them burst open, though, and through those seams, the seedy, jamlike inner flesh gleamed in the first light. The broken-open fruit attracted squirrels that scaled the limbs and hummingbirds that hovered, dipping needlelike beaks into the cracks to sip the sweet juices. We also found large, iridescent-green fig beetles that latched onto the overripe fruit where it had split; they stayed there all day, slowly feasting. It seemed that the tree was, in some way, feeding every insect or animal in the neighborhood.

Our hearts can, if we let them, oftentimes feel as soft and fragile as those figs. I remember that time in my life when I was homeless and jobless, staying in the spare rooms of friends and family. How open and humbled I was by the experience of having nowhere else to turn, living in fear because I had no idea what would come next. For someone who prided himself on accomplishment and success, the experience brought me to my knees and wore away so much of the tough skin I'd acquired. Each morning back then, I woke with the sense that my life had painfully split in two, but I could not have guessed that, later on, an undeniable sweetness would enter too, in the form of a stronger faith and a firmer commitment to my creativity, to offering my gifts to others.

Even now, I feel the same whenever I'm visiting my mother and have to drive her to a test at the hospital. While sitting in the waiting room, I watch the elderly man with a walker and tank of oxygen struggle toward a chair. I notice the young woman with an unnaturally ashen face digging anxiously in her purse for her insurance card. I see my mother's face grow redder and redder as we head to the car, as she struggles for the breath that comes so easily to me. I do not enjoy witnessing any of this, yet I must admit that each experience reminds me how temporary a healthy body can be. I am softened as I reluctantly accept that to give completely of myself, I must let my heart split open over and over so the sweetness inside can feed the world.

The Diamonds Inside

If you hide yourself away in the thickest woods how will your wisdom's light shine through?

—Hanshan

Staring in the mirror one morning, while examining my blemishes and brushing the flakes of dandruff from my shoulders, I had a revelation. I saw that I had always believed myself to be a fundamentally flawed human being with a body, a set of habits, and a heart not worthy of love. Though each man I dated taught me necessary lessons, I saw why I had always chosen the wrong ones as partners. My only goal had been to find someone willing to put up with all of what I perceived as my shortcomings—my quietness, my need for solitude, my small frame. I had never sought out another man who might support me in my creativity or on my spiritual path. It was no surprise that others could not love me at that time, since I had not yet learned to love myself.

That day I tapped into what Debbie Ford calls a "shadow belief," a deeply held yet unconscious conviction that governs everything we do and that keeps us from seeking out ways to share our gifts and express our whole selves. By buying into our shadow beliefs, we ourselves become shadows, beings that feed only on darkness or negativity and who are never nourished or full. Having always felt like an outsider and observer of life, I further separated myself from the world by believing that if anyone ever really got to know me, they would reject me. As a result, I chose partners who were misfits in the puzzle of my life so that when they inevitably broke things off, I would not have to feel as disappointed. Eventually, of course, the pain of such a strategy took its toll on my soul, and I went into hiding, refusing to date for almost five years and thereby guarding my heart from further harm.

I do not regret the string of ill-fitting partners or all the time I spent alone doing my best to heal and feel through my shadow beliefs and patterns. These choices brought me to that moment in front of the mirror when I looked into my own frightened eyes and saw the truth in a flash of self-love. It was as though I had a stash of diamonds all along that I refused to show anyone, believing they would not gleam enough if I lifted them out of the darkness where I'd kept them stored for so long. But that day, I suddenly knew I had to risk showing my gifts to others, opening up to them, so that all the facets of my being could catch the light, and give it back.

Waylaid

I was at the Getty Museum in Los Angeles with my friend Stella to see the famous Vermeer painting *Woman in Blue Reading a Letter*. When I stepped into the room where it was displayed, I felt a sense of deep quiet emanating from the canvas, which measured only about eighteen by fifteen inches. Though painted around 1663–1664, its colors still stood out as vivid and alive, depicting a young woman wearing a blue bedjacket and standing before a wide window, reading a letter while morning light bathed her whole body. Many believe the letter came from her lover and that her jacket hides the bulge of a secret pregnancy. But we will never know what Vermeer intended, for this woman with her parted lips and downcast eyes is still as mysterious to us as Leonardo's Mona Lisa.

I had wanted for years to see this painting in person, and once I'd spent more than an hour studying the luminous canvas, I felt that odd disappointment that sometimes comes after great anticipation and buildup. Perhaps there was a bit of self-pity as well, as I asked myself: Will I ever make anything so intricate, lasting, and lovely?

Waiting for Stella to finish up in the gift shop, I went and sat in the stone courtyard in the direct sunlight, feeling entirely open to the warmth of the world at that moment. Just then, I noticed two men unfolding a museum map, then speaking in sign language to one another. When they began to hold hands and stroll around the fountain, I knew they were lovers and couldn't help but be brought into the silence that seemed to envelop them. It was the silence of two people paying deep attention to and literally communicating with each other's bodies, the silence of partners who have been together for a long time and know each other inside and out. I watched as they traded pecks on the cheek before moving on, like mirror images of one another in their matching tennis shoes and black jackets.

Though I will always remember seeing the Vermeer, I felt more humbled by that couple's quiet presence with each other. In all relationships, after all, we are called to pay attention to the unsaid, to what cannot always be communicated with words spoken out loud. I had come to view a 350-year-old painting, but became waylaid and touched by a much more ordinary scene that has since followed me like a benediction, showing what's possible when we allow ourselves to know someone else and be known in the deepest ways.

Scraping Away

What love gives you is the courage to face the secrets you've kept from yourself, a reason to open the rest of the doors.

—Paul Monette

We become our most essential selves in the midst of strife. Like beech trees that give up their leaves only at the stubborn end of winter, we are all eventually stripped bare of those outer coverings we thought we'd always need for protection.

I remember the night Brad and I stood calmly cooking dinner, reheating leftover pasta and boiling sweet corn Brad had picked in the farm fields that morning. Little did he know, I was keeping a tally of what felt like slights and criticisms leveled at me throughout the day. I managed to hold my tongue, though, at least until he told me not to use the metal spoon in our already very worn pot, that it might scrape the bottom. My face turned red and began to burn. I rolled my eyes, laid a plastic spoon on the counter, and left the room so I could keep my cool—but it was no use. I felt I just had to make him aware of his "critical" behavior.

I blamed him at first, though after many heated words, I saw that his so-called criticisms were simply uncovering long-buried wounds from childhood, when I believed that achievement and perfection were the only ways to win affection, when I was so afraid of doing something wrong, I could hardly control my anxiety. We both lost our appetites that night, and it took days for me to stop feeling foolish and exposed for letting him know what was really bothering me, for being more vulnerable with another human being than I ever had been before. Yet I was also relieved this pain came to the surface and broke through at least part of my long-held armor. For it was in that moment that I began to be the kind of person who was willing to make mistakes, both large and small, without taking it personally when someone pointed them out, without believing my so-called mistakes and missteps made me a lesser human being.

It has been a slow and painful process, this stripping of layers in the name of greater intimacy with myself and others, but I know it is necessary for growth. There is no other choice. We must let the outer world scrape away our useless skins and masks so that our tender inner selves might at last shine through. So that when you look at me, and I look at you, we see the shiny pink scars that mean we are alive and learning.

Gold Can Stay

Even though the gold of your true nature can get buried beneath fear,
uncertainty, and confusion, the more you trust this loving presence as
the truth of who you are, the more fully you will call it forth in yourself
and in all those you touch.

—Tara Brach

When I first moved to Vermont to be with Brad, it felt like stepping off a
cliff into the unknown. I had never lived in the country before and had
expected that as a gay man, I would always be more comfortable in larger
cities. I left behind a teaching job at a community college in Boston that I
loved, along with a few good friends, and set about rebuilding a life from
scratch with no connections other than this man I had known for only six
months before we officially moved in together. I know the path of growth
almost always involves surrender, letting go, and rebirth. And those words
sound so inviting and enticing, until life insists we put them into practice.
In truth, the aftermath of my move left me feeling confused and raw, completely exposed and living in a world I hardly recognized.

One March evening, as Brad and I walked an old logging road up in the
woods behind our house, I finally confessed how much I was struggling to
make a new life here, all the trouble with finding a job. At the time, we lived
on part of the farm Brad helps to manage, and my solitude was constantly
disrupted by workers coming and going in the fields, by the rumbling
of tractors that readied the ground for planting. I thought about how
Brad's friends and family felt free to stop by our house, even if they knew
I was alone. Once, I'd been about to get in the shower (though luckily
still dressed) with a towel draped over my arm, when Brad's friend Greg
dropped by in the middle of the day just to grab a beer from the fridge,
taking a break from his round of deliveries to have a drink out on our
picnic bench. Then I remembered all the rejections I'd gotten from local
colleges and universities, even for positions for which I was overqualified.

I felt hopeless, at the end of my rope, and trapped in a house that didn't feel like my own.

"Babe," Brad said after I poured out my heart. "The universe doesn't even know where you are yet. You just got here. Give yourself some time."

He promised he would talk to everyone and let them know I needed my space, as strange as it might seem to them. He also said that, for now at least, I didn't need to worry about money or fear that I wasn't contributing enough—not easy for a chronic overachiever to hear. Yet his kind, reassuring words allowed me to take my first deep breath of the past few weeks.

Give yourself some time was exactly the permission I needed during this period of finding my way. I had always been a driven person, constantly reaching for this or that goal, and in this new place without a regular job, I felt like a failure, like I'd made a mistake in giving everything up to follow my heart, even though it had felt like the only right thing to do. We often forget that it takes time to adjust to new circumstances, to bring about larger change in our lives. We expect immediate results once we've made certain shifts, neglecting to bring the necessary gentleness and patience to the process. In my own life up to that point, I had just moved on from place to place and job to job when I didn't get the results I wanted or when I started to feel bored. But that was no longer an option now, since I had made a commitment to being here with this man I loved.

As we started back to the house, I looked down at the gravel trail and saw a single beech leaf splayed there and shining at the edges as if it had been dipped briefly in gold. As I'd learned that past winter, beech trees hold onto their leaves until the last possible moment, until new buds on the branches finally force them to let go. The way that leaf shone in the day's fading light felt like the glimmer of hope Brad had just given me, the indestructible kindness of someone who finally trusted and believed in me. It made me think of Robert Frost's famous line: "Nothing gold can stay." But his words rang suddenly false to me then. True, the leaf would soon break down and return to earth again, but doesn't the gold of it still live in me the same way Brad's words of permission would carry me through the rest of that evening and the difficulties of my transition into a brand-new life? Doesn't the gold of kindness always stay with us over the years, a bright and priceless presence we turn to again and again?

Wild Geraniums

We have a half-mile forest trail by our house that almost no one uses. I can be alone as I walk it, back and forth, often working out some creative or emotional problem. I simply walk among the trees, trying not to step on the tiny orange newts who stretch out across the wet stones on the path, often startling the chipmunks back into their holes in the old stone walls. By the time I'm finished, whatever mood had held me in its grips has usually passed through, and I can see my world with the fresh eyes of kindness and an open heart again. One summer morning, though, the feeling was strong: I no longer wanted to live here in Vermont, tucked deep in the woods, hours away from culture and decent food. I longed for the ease of the city, takeout Cambodian, cups of espresso sipped at a sidewalk café, supermarkets with anything I wanted just a short walk away. Never mind that as soon as I set foot in a city, a new litany of complaints starts up about the noise of other people in the apartment building where I'm staying, the constant thrum of traffic, and the sirens of emergency vehicles wailing day and night.

If we're not careful, we can spend whole chunks of our lives wishing to be elsewhere, instead of letting gratitude guide us back to where we are now, to all that's worthy of love right here. I have always been a victim of the kind of thinking that I call "grass is greener mentality." Instead of sinking deeply into the present moment of where I find myself and embracing all the beauty and inevitable flaws, I focus on some other, better time to come in the future. The result, of course, is that I miss out on the abundance that's almost always available to me here and now.

By my fourth loop on the trail in the woods, I was beginning to feel at least some appreciation, glad to be alone in the green light of trees surrounding me on all sides, seeing the white and purple asters beginning to bloom. I also noticed what Brad had recently told me were wild geraniums sprouting up everywhere beside the path, with their constellations of tiny pink blossoms—so bright in the shadows—and feather-soft leaves. Then I saw a clump of it literally growing out of the side of an old maple, having taken root in the carpet of moss wrapped around its wide and gnarled trunk. I knelt down to get a better look and shook my head, marveling at the resilience and stubbornness of nature. And I thought, if this wild geranium can thrive here in a clump of moss, then I can grow anywhere I'm planted, too. It might not look like it from the outside, but perhaps that is the perfect place for the plant; maybe it has found exactly what it needs, all the nutrients and water it takes to bloom.

In a way, we are all like wild geraniums, with so little control over where our lives carry us, or what circumstances we're placed in. Who's to say we can't find solid ground wherever we are, even if we sense that this place is not permanent? Why not absorb what we can and grow where we are, letting ourselves be fed by a life that might at times feel less than ideal? I came home that morning still moody and unmotivated, but nevertheless more grateful for my place on the planet than I had been in weeks. Years ago, I would have chided myself—which never helps—for not owning my privilege and the beauty of this life we've built surrounded by woods. I would have tried to berate myself into a feeling of gratitude, which also never works. Instead, I headed outdoors, trying not to force any insights, but ready to receive what the world had to offer me. And nature repaid that openness with the kindness of wild geraniums springing miraculously from the side of the tree as if to teach me: this is how you grow, no matter your own resistance, no matter what you're given.

KiNDNESS PRACTiCE

STOPPING FOR BEAUTY

How often have I refused to pause in my daily busyness to take in some bit of beauty, to let a sense of wonder for this world take over my heart and mind? We get so caught up in our lives, bowing under the weighty pressures of time and obligation, that we forget to notice those who might need our help, forget to look beneath the surface of the outer masks we all present to each other, to see what lies beneath. As meditation teacher Tara Brach has written: "Focusing on our own concerns and stress can put us in a trance, covering over our natural sensitivity and compassion." Locked in such a trance, we become unavailable to the beauty of people and other beings around us, missing out on chances to offer them the gift of our attention. We also lose compassion and kindness for ourselves when we allow the pressures of responsibility to dictate our every move, telling ourselves the story that we don't have time to swerve from our goals to feed our joy or appreciate some stunning aspect of nature.

We may not always have the luxury to pause, but when we miss those opportunities, we can carry regret with us for years to come. Once, I ran into a neighbor at a local bookstore, and my intuition told me that something was wrong, that she needed to talk. This only occurred to me after we had parted ways, yet instead of seeking her out again and offering to sit down together, I told myself I had to get home and finish my work for the day. Another time, driving back from a visit with my mother, I saw a flock of hundreds of snowy geese in a field by the side of the highway in Missouri, where they had stopped to rest on their long migration. I saw other drivers pulling onto the shoulder to snap photos, and while I knew I didn't need snapshots to remember them, I still felt the call to stop in the middle of that eight-hour drive and just stand there, taking in the rare scene of these wondrous birds gathered together in one place. I was on a schedule, I told myself, and couldn't afford those few extra minutes. Though I've since forgiven myself for rushing past beauty, these missed chances serve as reminders of the price for not pausing, for not giving myself the kindness of that time to savor the world we live in or connect with a friend.

Invitation for Writing & Reflection

Think back to a time when you failed to stop for some bit of beauty or wonder that you wanted to savor. What story did you tell yourself and how might you make more room in your life for future pauses, for the gratitude that can lead to a fuller presence and kindness toward everyone you meet?

Perennials

Driving by the yards of abandoned farmhouses all across Vermont, I often see evidence of their former inhabitants in the form of daylilies, daisies, and irises still blooming among the tall, uncut grass. I have heard others call these patches "ghost gardens" because the perennials keep coming back year after year with their profusion of scents and colors, even without any humans to tend them. Surely the hands that placed those plants and bulbs in the ground never imagined that decades, or perhaps even hundreds of years later, people would still be enjoying the fruits of their attentive labor.

Many of us worry that our own actions are pointless, that we may never affect the lives of others in a positive way. We cannot know the full outcome of most of what we do, the power of small actions taken daily for the betterment of the world. Yet this much is true: Whatever seeds we sow in others and in ourselves, whatever we plant and care for in the present moment, will *always* return in some way, shape, or form down the road—whether we're there to witness it, or not. It is a law of the universe that no amount of energy we expend in bringing something loving or creative into this world is ever wasted. Whoever planted the tiger lilies I saw blazing in the spring sun as I drove by a fallen-in old barn the other day had no idea that some future stranger would be so moved by the sight of them he would pull off the dirt road in the middle of a day to take a photo. They could not know I would carry the sudden pleasure of that sighting with me; they simply planted the flowers for their own enjoyment and trusted that their joy was enough.

Those of us who teach or raise children or look after the sick or dying—which is to say, all of us at some point in our lives—will sow the seeds of love and attention, though we may never see or feel the results of our efforts. A wide-ranging faith allows us to look beyond the now, beyond the doubt and fear, to a time when our love will have assembled a life of its own. I have been lucky enough to feel this with my writing, when people tell me how my work has added to their own memories or perceptions and how they have shared my books and teachings with others. The energy from any generative or kind act continues to ripple out and reach toward others, whether as a ghost garden, a quilt that will be passed through the generations, or a painting sold at a tag sale that will be hung and cherished by someone who remains a stranger to the painter. As long as we are offering something with a full heart, we can trust that anything we give will surely outlive us.

Wait and See

Sometimes grace is a ribbon of mountain air that gets in through the cracks.

—Anne Lamott

Recently, Brad was explaining to me a rather inelegant term they use here on the farm. Whenever the clouds part just enough to reveal blue sky and sunshine on an otherwise gray day, they call it a "sucker hole." This is because, as a farmer, if you think that brief glimpse of light means it's going to be a sunny and warm day all of a sudden, you might end up rushing around to all your greenhouses, watering the plants just beginning to sprout and grow in spring. Yet, if it turns out that the hole in the clouds was just that, and decided to close up, you will not only have wasted precious time on a useless task, you might also overwater and kill your plants.

I asked him how to avoid this.

"You just have to wait and see," he said.

This speaks to so many aspects of life and relationships. With only the barest of evidence, it can be easy to start telling ourselves stories about how things are, or how they will be. Even though I spend about an hour a day in meditation, trying to watch and label my runaway thoughts, the seduction of making up stories to explain the world and my reactions remains so enticing. A series of missteps in the morning—spilled coffee, an angry email—might convince me it's just going to be one of those days, but only if I make the decision to let it become that way. Only if I refuse to wait and see. This used to happen to me all the time in relationships with others. I'd see a ray of light or two, a glimpse of kindness or romance in a friend or partner who was not right for me, and I'd use that hint to create a version of that person in my mind that simply wasn't true. In a way, fantasy is always more inviting, and even briefly satisfying at times, because we're the ones pulling the strings, making it up as we go. It gives us a false sense of control, but it's about as nourishing as fast food, which never fulfills us in the end because it's not quite real.

As Brad pointed out, just by cultivating the kindness of our patience, and not coming to any conclusions right away, we save ourselves from wasting time and effort on the useless task of tending to something or someone that isn't for us.

Hurry

Just the other day, I'd fallen again into the usual rush of a day full of obligations. But by the time I reached the crowded checkout lines at the grocery store and saw the overloaded cart of the woman in front of me, I knew I'd have to wait, whether I wanted to or not. As I stood scanning the magazines full of recipes and celebrity news, I began to wonder about what I was rushing toward in the first place. I thought about the poem "Hurry" by Marie Howe, in which she keeps pushing her young daughter to speed through their errands. Finally, she asks: "Where do I want her to hurry to? To her grave? To mine?" Perhaps only a poet could get away with asking such a bold and essential question of herself.

I had bought into the false story that I needed to hurry because I had so much to do that morning and thought I couldn't make time for the slowness I've learned is my own basic nature. Breathing more peacefully, I began to give my attention to the world around me again, noticing the woman's groceries ahead of me—cases of Gatorade, slabs of frozen ribs—and eavesdropping on her conversation with the young woman bagging her items, who I soon saw was a girl with special needs. Yet this young girl was performing the magic of drawing everyone around her—worker and customer alike—into closer relationships with each other.

"You see that woman over there?" she asked the customer ahead of me, pointing to another checker. "My birthday's coming up, and she's gonna make me a giraffe cake. She's doing her research right now so she gets it just right."

We all smiled, feeling the grace of this exchange, our own sympathetic joy sparked by her excitement for an upcoming birthday. I felt amazed by how I'd been fooled once again by those stories scrolling through my head, telling me to push on to the next thing and the next. Simply by waiting, I watched the heavy clouds that had hung over my morning part fully during that shared moment in the fluorescent glare of the supermarket.

The World Right Here

Love wakens the world.

—Anya Silver

What if heaven for us is every moment we give in to love, instead of fear? What if our purpose here is simply to keep this mysterious force we call love from going extinct, by choosing to preserve it as often as possible, even when our minds crave the darker, more familiar feelings of blame and worry?

Yesterday, Brad was trying to carry too much from the car into the house. His arms were piled with jackets, books, and the two jars of honey we had purchased from the beekeeper just down the street. I was rushing inside because I didn't feel well, but paused and turned around when I heard Brad jokingly say: "Don't worry, I'll get it all." As soon as those words came out of his mouth, one of the jars fell to the driveway and shattered. Five pounds of sweet, precious, amber-colored honey began spreading out over the gravel, seeping into the ground. "*Honey,*" I said to him almost sternly, no pun intended, but then I caught myself. I was about to chide him for what was simply an accident. I had a flash of empathy as it dawned on me just how awful I would feel if this had happened to me. Brad and I both have a tendency to beat ourselves up over accidents and mistakes (we are recovering perfectionists), but, luckily, that insight slipped into my mind before I spoke another harsh word to him.

At first, I had wanted to blame him for trying to do too much by himself, another old habit, for bringing things inside that could have just stayed in the car until later. But why do we think that blame and shame will ever solve anything or change someone's behavior? I often fail to step into another's shoes even for a few minutes and let the holy *aha* take over—suddenly sensing how they must be feeling and deciding not to add to their suffering or the suffering of the world with my aggression. "I'm so sorry," I said to Brad, putting down the bag I was carrying. I went over to where he stood, staring down dejectedly at the widening puddle of honey. "Oh, well," I said. "It's no big deal."

It took him hours to be able to crack a smile about what had happened, to stop shaming himself. "Do you know how much work goes into making five pounds of honey?" he asked, having finished picking up the shards of glass and cleaning up what he could, leaving the rest for the ants. I had no answer; I just opened my arms and held him for as long as I could. My flash of empathy told me that what he was feeling was *not* about the broken jar or spilled honey or wasted money and effort. He was being offered a chance to forgive himself and accept that accidents happen to all of us.

It can feel like a radical choice—to move toward love instead of blaming others, instead of shaming ourselves for something we could not prevent. Yet, the centering force of love always breaks the cycle of suffering in the moment and, eventually, in our larger lives. Love turns our attention from the broken, from the shards of what we've done in the past, or what's been done to us, toward the wholeness of the world right here. Love outlasts all accidents, failures, mistakes, and wrong turns—like honey itself, which remains sweet, edible, and delicious even hundreds of years after it's been pulled from the hive and poured into jars.

Pieces of Heaven

We had gone away for a week with my mother-in-law, Ann, to a small house on the coast of Maine, perched at the edge of the Muscongus Sound. After such a full year of building and moving into our new house, then transitioning out of several jobs, and heading back to the Midwest to see my mother and other relatives, it was a relief to have reached a still point, to be in a place where the main event was the sunrise each morning. Brad and I would wake early at five, make coffee and toast, then sit on the couch with the lights off while the sun slowly rose over a tree-lined island in the distance, filling the sky with yellow, then violet, then pink, and turning the placid water that same color as loons floated in with their haunting calls and the occasional head of a seal broke surface.

This annual trip is one of the few indulgences my mother-in-law allows herself, as she works hard throughout the year, caring for children and cleaning houses, saving every dollar for this week when we can all escape together. It can be a lot of pressure to place on a vacation, to *expect* rest and recharge from a single week away from the stresses of life, yet I enjoy each year watching how she relishes the moments, buying herself an extra apple turnover and blueberry scone from the bakery we walk to each morning, insisting on treating us to T-shirts and mugs if we show the slightest interest in them. "So you guys can remember this time," she always says.

But during this trip, it dawned on me just how much she makes a practice of gratitude for this time, tending to those bits of beauty she allows herself, what the poet William Stafford called "pieces of heaven." While she and Brad were out for a walk, I happened to pass by her bedroom and noticed the bouquet of tulips she'd gotten for herself resting on the carpet. Why were her flowers on the floor? We had chuckled at her at the start of our stay when she came out of the grocery store clutching the yellow and orange tulips pressed to her chest like a prized possession, plastic crinkling as she climbed in the car, unable to contain her excitement at having found them. When we got back to the rental house, she searched every cabinet for the perfect vase to display them, settling on an old crock that she filled with water and placed on the living room table.

As it turns out, she had moved them out of the full and surprisingly strong November sun and into the cooler shadows of her bedroom floor just so they would last a little longer. I smiled to myself, thinking: Who does that? But with admiration for the attention she gives to such seemingly small things. Most of us, myself included at times, might buy or pick some flowers, find a place for them, and then forget them until they began to fade and wilt and drop their petals. Each day, my mother-in-law lifted the crock from the table and laid it on the rug in her bedroom, treating that bundle of beauty as a precious commodity she might never get to experience again. What might have seemed like a lot of trouble to go to for a grocery-store bouquet of tulips suddenly seemed to me an act of love and care, mindfulness and presence. She wanted us all to keep on appreciating the tulips as they opened their petals a little more every day, each one like a cup tenderly shaped to hold the light it's been given.

Acknowledgments

I've said it before, and I'll say it again: my husband, Brad Peacock, has taught me more about kindness than I ever thought possible. This book would not exist without him and his compassionate example in the world. Other inspirations and examples of kindness include: Ted Kooser, Naomi Shihab Nye, Danusha Laméris, Rosemerry Wahtola Trommer, Ross Gay, Elizabeth Berg, Tara Brach, Anne Lamott, and Mark Nepo. Huge thanks to my amazing agent, Gareth Esersky, for believing in this project from the beginning and shepherding it from a very rough draft into an actual book. The team at Weldon Owen/Insight Editions has been a dream to work with; endless thanks to Katie Killebrew, Karyn Gerhard, Margaret Parrish, Amanda Nelson, Roger Shaw, Raoul Goff, and everyone who helped to bring this book into the world. Immense gratitude to Dinara Mirtalipova for her gorgeous artwork and yet another wondrous cover. I also want to thank the staff and teachers at the Insight Meditation Society in Barre, Massachusetts, for their dedication to meditation and mindfulness practice, and for providing a space of kindness for those on the spiritual path. Finally, I thank everyone (some are strangers) who helped to spark these essays or gave essential support, especially: Kim Hays, Amanda Noska, Ann and Duane Peacock, Diane Peacock, Erin Peacock, Michelle Wiegers, Cindy Crews, Ron Crews, Freddie Crews, Gaetane and Alexandra Pell, Wassim Nehme, Beth Newman, Heather Swan, Stella Nelson, Andrew Knafel, Anne Hunter, Christy Nevius, Erin Quick, Shari Altman, Shari Stenberg, Shannon Darnell, Linda West, Lynn Weiss, my late grandmother, Mary Ann White, and my late father, James Crews Sr., whose love and kindness underpin every word I write.

MANDALA

An Imprint of MandalaEarth
PO Box 3088
San Rafael, CA 94912
www.MandalaEarth.com

 Find us on Facebook: www.facebook.com/MandalaEarth
Follow us on Twitter: @MandalaEarth

CEO Raoul Goff
Associate Publisher Phillip Jones
Editorial Director Katie Killebrew
Senior Editor Karyn Gerhard
VP Creative Chrissy Kwasnik
Art Director Ashley Quackenbush
Production Designer Jean Hwang
VP Manufacturing Alix Nicholaeff
Production Manager Joshua Smith
Sr Production Manager, Subsidiary Rights Lina s Palma-Temena

MandalaEarth would also like to thank Margaret Parrish and Bob Cooper for their work on this book.

ISBN: 979-8-88762-000-8

Manufactured in China by Insight Editions
10 9 8 7 6 5 4 3 2 1

Insight Editions, in association with Roots of Peace, will plant two trees for each tree used in the manufacturing of this book. Roots of Peace is an internationally renowned humanitarian organization dedicated to eradicating land mines worldwide and converting war-torn lands into productive farms and wildlife habitats. Roots of Peace will plant two million fruit and nut trees in Afghanistan and provide farmers there with the skills and support necessary for sustainable land use.